NOTES TO SELF

'A heartfelt, beautifully written collection . . . Running like a thread through it all is anger, then relief, as she finds the courage to set down what she wants to say. There is so much here worth saying that one only hopes Pine has a longer book in her.'

—*Herald*

'It would be hard to find writing more powerful than that in these essays. These are notes for everyone.'

—*Image Magazine*

'. . . you wish you could have read her words sooner. Every woman has that writer that makes them feel less alone in their own bodies, who, through their refusal to be silent about insecurity and embarrassment, answers the clawing question "is it just me who feels like this?" Emilie Pine is that writer.'

—*Totally Dublin*

'Poignant, brave, at once highly personal and consciously representative.'

—*Cara Magazine*

ABOUT THE AUTHOR

Emilie Pine is Associate Professor of Modern Drama at University College Dublin, Ireland. She has published widely as an academic and critic. *Notes to Self* is her first collection of personal essays and the winner of the Butler Literary Award, the *Sunday Independent* Newcomer of the Year Award, and Book of the Year 2018 at the Irish Book Awards.

NOTES TO SELF

Essays

Emilie Pine

PENGUIN BOOKS

PENGUIN BOOKS

UK | USA | Canada | Ireland | Australia
India | New Zealand | South Africa

Penguin Books is part of the Penguin Random House group of companies
whose addresses can be found at global.penguinrandomhouse.com.

First published in the Republic of Ireland by Tramp Press 2018
First published in Great Britain by Hamish Hamilton 2019
Published in Penguin Books 2019

002

Copyright © Emilie Pine, 2018

The moral right of the author has been asserted

Set in 13.6/16 pt Fournier MT Std
Typeset by Jouve (UK), Milton Keynes
Printed and bound in Great Britain by Clays Ltd, Elcograf S.p.A.

A CIP catalogue record for this book is available from the British Library

ISBN: 978-0-241-98622-6

www.greenpenguin.co.uk

for Ronan

Contents

xi

NOTES TO SELF

NOTES ON
INTEMPERANCE

BY THE TIME WE FIND HIM, he has been lying in a small pool of his own shit for several hours.

Corfu General Hospital is bewildering. The foyer is crowded with patients smoking, and there is no sign of an information or registration desk. I text him to ask where he is but get no response. Somehow, like blood-hounds, we track him to the fifth floor. He lies weakly in the bed. It is evening now and he says he hasn't seen a nurse or doctor since midday. He says he needs a bedpan. My sister and I have been travelling for over twenty-four hours, and neither of us has slept. 'Call the nurse,' I tell him. He says he did, but nothing happened.

'Well, do it again.' He holds the call bell in his hand and presses, repeatedly. After a while a harassed-looking nurse appears, shouting at him, at us. I feel guilty for not speaking Greek. With useless gestures, I point to the man in the bed, I try to signal that he needs a bedpan, to be washed, and the sheets changed. None of this makes any impression. The nurse says something else, throws up her hands and leaves. He looks at us in desperation. I ask my sister to stay with him and I go out into the corridor. I can see only other patients, and their families. I go to the nurses' station but there is no one there. As I walk away, at a loss for what to do, a woman speaks to me. When I don't respond, she asks me in English if I am alright and I latch on, asking her if she knows where the nurses are. 'There are no nurses,' she tells me. An older man leans over. 'Without your family here, you die.'

This will become a mantra to us during the time that we spend in Greece, trying to nurse our father back to life. Very quickly we learn just how understaffed the hospital is. There are no doctors after 2pm, and after 5pm there is only one nurse per ward. On this corridor, I count six rooms, each with up to six patients. The nurse is barely able to cover the basic medical needs of all these people, and she does not have time to deal with incontinence. We also learn that this floor – officially for

4

patients requiring 'internal medicine' – is dubbed 'the dying ward'.

The English-speaking local tells me that I must take care of my father. She explains gently where to buy incontinence pads and wipes and paper towels. I barely take this in, but go back into the private room my father's crisis status has secured him, and explain to my sister the state of play. She looks at me in disbelief. She is standing at the head of Dad's bed, and fixing his pillows. I realise that I have hardly spoken to him, though I have travelled across Europe to be here. 'You're alive anyway,' I say. He nods. He looks very small in the bed, small and lost. I decide that this can't be the way it is – there must be someone in authority somewhere in this hospital. I go back into the corridor and ask the sympathetic woman if she will help me to find a doctor. She talks quickly with her family and then walks off down the corridor, with me following. We take a lift to another floor, but there are no doctors there. We get back in the lift and try again. We do this over and over, down and down, until we're in the basement, searching its corridors. Eventually we find the blood donation clinic with its attending medic. My new friend ushers me in, then waves goodbye.

On the far side of the room, a man is lying on a couch, his sleeve rolled up and his arm attached to an IV. He is giving blood, and the clinic attendant seems to think I am there to donate too. Seeing my surprise, the doctor explains to me that there is a national blood shortage in Greece, and it is law that patients' families give blood. I think of my sister, five floors above, wondering where I am. I shake my head, but the words won't come. I can't seem to explain in any language that we are both anaemic and unable to give blood. I take his hand and ask him to see my father. I tell him that I don't understand, that my father is alone in a room and there are no doctors. I tell him that we just need someone to explain it all, though what I really want is someone to tell me what to do. The jolt of adrenaline which propelled me this far has suddenly gone and all I feel is empty. I just keep standing there, asking the doctor to come to see my father. Extremely reluctantly, he says something to the woman at the desk, and leaves the clinic. We take the lift back up to the fifth floor, retracing my route past the doleful visitors and into the room.

'He's a doctor,' I say, with more hope than certainty. He takes Dad's chart, looks it over, nodding, then says, 'Your father has lost a lot of blood. He will need transfusions. You must give blood.' It seems easier to agree, though I had hoped for a more thorough examination. In the weeks that follow, this will be the pattern that our time takes: hours of waiting, followed by a struggle to attract official attention, only to be told something that we already know. After years of teaching Beckett plays, I am finally living in one.

Having delivered his pronouncement, the doctor nods again and leaves. In his wake, I look to my father for guidance, but he only looks back at me for a reassurance I cannot give. I try to smile. We've now been here for more than an hour and though I know he is relieved to see us, and my sister has stroked his hand and made him feel much less alone, he is still lying in dirty sheets. Since no one else is going to help us, I ask my sister to come with me. 'We'll be back soon.' Downstairs we find the hospital shop, which sells a useful combination of hot snacks and drinks, and the products necessary for looking after a patient. We buy wipes and pads and, as an afterthought, my sister buys a box of surgical gloves. These, it turns out, will prove invaluable.

When we explain to Dad what we are going to do, he is distressed and embarrassed. But the smell in the room is now awful, and it drives us to be as efficient and business-like as we can. We clean him. Once the dirty sheets are bundled up, I take them to what looks like a utility room and guiltily leave them there. In an abandoned-seeming ward, I take clean sheets from one bed, and blankets from another, figuring that if you don't take, you don't get. When I come back into the room, my sister has managed to make Dad laugh. As we tuck the new sheets around him, it becomes clear how much our sense of humanity depends on these basic things. Nothing has really changed, and I am no clearer on Dad's exact medical status, but it feels as if we have achieved something huge.

It gets late. We agree that I will stay in the hospital overnight, and my sister will go to a hotel in town. I want to go with her, but from now on we will take it in turns to stay with Dad. She makes it out of the ward just in time – they lock the doors at 11pm. It is accepted that family members will stay, but the door prevents coming and going. After hugging her goodbye, I turn back to the room. I don't envy my sister her solitary journey to find a place to stay, but neither have I any idea how to navigate the night ahead in the hospital. Dad has slipped into unconsciousness. I listen to his breathing, hold my hand on his chest to feel his heart, which beats steadily, though it feels very faint. The bag of blood hanging by his head is now almost empty. I eye it warily, thinking that I don't have the energy to figure out what to do once it is gone. I dial the number for his insurance company but only get an automated message. When I realise that I have left my charger in my sister's bag, I give up the idea of phoning anyone else.

I turn off the lights and look out the window at the

hills north of the hospital, and listen as the late night quiet spreads through the ward. It gets so cold that I heap blankets on Dad. I sit in my coat and wait. After a while, the door opens and the harassed nurse re-enters. I watch silently as she takes down the empty blood bag, replaces it with a fresh one and squeezes to check that it is going in. She is wearing an apron that would look suitable on a butcher in an abattoir. It is only after she leaves that I realise she did not wear surgical gloves or wash her hands.

Later in the night, a different nurse appears and I manage to smile and proffer the box of gloves. She cautiously takes a pair and puts them in her pocket. 'No, no,' I say, smiling ingratiatingly. I mime for her to put them on but she only waggles her fingers to show she is already wearing gloves. Her pair, though, have blood and stains on them, and I mime for her to remove them and use the fresh ones. All this miming must seem ridiculous, but like the madwoman she presumably takes me for, I keep going until she sighs and changes the gloves. The old ones go in her pocket. This only becomes comprehensible several days later when another visitor explains that the hospital provides no disposable products at all – no cotton wool, no paper, no plastic. The nurses have to buy their own supplies, out of wages that are already insufficient. The glove pantomime becomes a regular occurrence and every time I give a nurse a fresh pair I feel like crying.

But that first night, as I half dozed, half listened anxiously for my father to take his next breath, I was too stunned to cry. I had expected the call for years, and had imagined the scenarios, so that when it came I was able to react, to make the necessary decisions. It was only in the quiet and the dark of the hospital room that I understood the call was only the beginning.

I HEAR THE BEEP, too early on a Sunday morning to be a casual message. The text reads: 'Am bledng. Dont fon'. I phone him. He sounds awful. He sounds like what he is: a man who is bleeding to death. He chokes and coughs, only barely able to speak, as the blood vomits out of him. I tell him to hold on. I ring his friend P, who lives on the other side of the island, and she rings the ambulance. But the driver refuses to go out on the call. He is spending Sunday with his family. He seems to think that it will be a wasted journey, that my dad will be dead already, and so he can wait until Monday. P berates and cajoles. It takes a long time for her and her husband to persuade the driver that despite it being a Sunday, and despite it being an hour's drive, he has to go. P doesn't tell me any of this until later. For now, she only makes me promise to ensure that Dad's front door is open. If the door is locked, they will leave again. I phone Dad back. He is, luckily, still conscious, and he crawls to the door, and turns the key in the lock. When the ambulance gets to his village, his neighbours direct them to his house. The emergency crew pick him up from the floor where he lies, now unconscious, and take him to the hospital.

In winter there are no direct flights from Ireland to Greece. Hours after the call, my sister and I fly from Dublin to Heathrow for our first stopover. Men in scarves crowd the plane, and I realise there must be some important football match on. At the new Terminal Four we eat in an Italian restaurant. Though it is grotesque to care about food while your father lies dying, I order truffle pasta and it is delicious.

Over dinner I tell my sister that I don't know what we will find when we get to Greece. I tell her that I am tired. I tell her about one evening several years earlier when I asked Dad to stop drinking. About how he poured himself another glass of wine as I was speaking. About how I was crying and he was telling me to stop being so stupid. I tell her that I threatened him, that I told him I would stop loving him. I tell her, though I am barely able to admit it to myself, that at one point that night I looked at him and thought, 'Just die now.'

As we eat and talk we keep checking our phones, a reflex that is both hopeful and fearful. We haven't heard from him since he was taken to hospital and we both know that he may be dead. My phone beeps, and I grab for it, but it's just an automatic update. My sister looks at me. She knows I could never stop loving him. The next morning we take the first plane to Athens, where we transfer to a flight to Corfu.

THEY CALL HIM 'THE CORPSE'. He's attached to machines that monitor his heart and other major organs. He has two IV lines, though the nurses struggle to find a vein that will take them as he has lost so much blood. He is barely awake most of the time. We're oblivious to his nickname until a Greek visitor lets us in on the joke. Typically, as with most things concerning Dad, it's both funny and not funny. Nobody, not even the nurses, thinks he's going to live through this. And yet – he refuses to die. After a week in the main hospital, on this end-of-life ward, where one or other of us is with him night and day, he's deemed stable enough to withstand a transfer to the 'English' clinic, which translates, basically, as 'clinic for people with health insurance'. It's a huge improvement: there are two nurses per shift and half the number of patients. Dad is bathed for the first time and the nurses insert a catheter. They don't see it as the family's duty to supply and oversee bedpans.

Each day we arrive at the clinic at 11am, stay till 5pm, leave for food, then come back for another few hours. We sit side-by-side and watch him, for hours, barely talking ourselves, just monitoring the man in the bed; we still expect him to die and we stay with him constantly, as if willing him to live will make a difference. The long hours are broken by a series of brief and frustrating conversations with elusive doctors. They cursorily examine him, then pronounce that we should take him back to Ireland. After all, they say, Ireland is a better country to have liver disease in, the doctors have plenty of experience, we're told, 'over there'.

Dad is in full liver failure. For years his other organs have been compensating for his diminished liver capacity. Now, after four decades of alcoholism, his system is shutting down. I had always assumed it would be cirrhosis that would end his life, but it turns out there's a host of other deadly illnesses to grapple with. The bleeding, from a rupture in his oesophagus, though it has almost killed him, is only the most obvious symptom. I remember an earlier sign of this: Dad stopping the car one day to retch and spit blood by the side of the road. Now his kidneys are also critical. The specialist tells us, though, that his heart is still in good shape. 'Perhaps medically speaking,' I want to say.

After a week, the doctors decide his oesophagus is sufficiently healed. They allow him to eat soft, plain food. But he won't eat. Or he won't eat what's on offer: eggs.

'I don't like eggs.'

'You have to eat.'

'But you know I don't like eggs.'

'I don't care, you have to eat.'

This role reversal, with the child feeding the parent, is bitterly ironic. We are all here because he likes to drink and now he has the temerity to refuse to eat. We do a deal. If he eats one hardboiled egg, I will buy him pens and paper. Later I promise a stapler too if he eats a second egg. Because he is a writer, he feels insecure without the means of writing things down and organising them. He gives me animated and detailed descriptions of where to buy these essential supplies. Yet, in the end, he only eats half of one egg.

No stapler, I tell him.

He doesn't speak to me for an entire day.

*

Neil phones me every day, sometimes twice a day; his is one of the few numbers I can answer easily. Neil is Dad's best friend. When Dad is refusing to eat, or the insurance company says that they won't pay the bill for the private clinic, or the doctor says Dad is probably going to die, I fear I will cry out in pain. But then the phone rings and it's Neil, and as I listen to his reassuringly buoyant voice I begin to think it'll be okay. He asks about Dad, about the doctors, he makes me feel like we can get through this. He knows that, from Dublin, there's little he can do, and he knows that phoning me cannot change the doctors' prognosis. But he also knows that this daily call is what I need. Neil gives me the number of a doctor friend in Ireland who will translate what the Greek doctors are saying. I phone this friend and describe Dad's condition, his list of ailments. He tells me to get Dad home. *Now.*

Z, Y, X, W, V . . .

That's how I was taught the alphabet. 'My five-year-old daughter can say the alphabet backwards faster than you.' That's how it went, the bet. I was taken out of bed, and brought downstairs to perform the feat in front of a tableful of drunk grown-ups. The bet was won, I was returned to bed. Why my dad chose to teach me the alphabet backwards I don't know – I've asked him, and he doesn't know either. I put it down to the fact that he likes to stand at an angle to the world, that for him to follow the standard rule of *a, b, c* seems oppressively normal, and that, as his first child, I was fallow ground for testing his theories. And I was a quick study. Because above all else, I wanted to be like – and to be liked by – my dad. Nowadays, when I'm filing student record cards, I still mix it up – is it *p, q, r* or *r, q, p*?

Dad's unusual approach to parenting was not limited to the alphabet. When I was four years old, he took me to the beach. I made sandcastles by myself, while he sat on a folding chair, reading. He had not packed a picnic, so when I said I was hungry, he sent me to find some other children in the hope that their parents would feed me. It worked. To this day, Dad tells this anecdote as a sign of his ingenuity. He has never been shy about sharing how happy he is to relinquish the duty of care towards his children.

As we grew up, we knew not to ask anything of him. When I was ten years old, Dad left us in a pub. He was angry because I hadn't stopped my five-year-old sister from pouring her orange squash into his gin and tonic. He drove away and he did not come back for us. We

found someone else to give us dinner. We found some-
one else to drive us home. We put ourselves to bed.
These did not feel like out-of-the-ordinary things to
have to do. Like all children of heavy drinkers, we
developed a particular kind of watchfulness. We learned,
through experience, not to trust. We learned to cope
with crisis. And if ever we put ourselves in his way he
would say the most creatively hurtful things. When I
became a teenager he started calling me a 'slut', which,
in his special way, could be wielded as both an insult
and a compliment.

It is hard to love an addict. Not only practically diffi-
cult, in the picking up after them and the handling of
those aspects of life they're not able for themselves, but
metaphysically hard. It feels like bashing yourself against
a wall, not just your head, but your whole self. It makes
your heart hard. Caught between endless ultimatums
(stop drinking) and radical acceptance (I love you no
matter what) the person who loves the addict exhausts
and renews their love on a daily basis. I used to push
myself to reject him, to walk away, failing each time. I
oscillated between caring for the man who was afflicted
with this terrible disease, and attempting to protect
myself from the emotional fallout of having an alcoholic
father. It took years of refusing him empathy before I
realised that the only person I was hurting was myself.

When I was in my twenties, Dad moved to Greece. I put him in the taxi that took him to the airport, aware as I waved him off of the irony that it is usually children, not parents, who leave for a new life elsewhere. As I waved, I smiled, but I was heart-sore. Since the break-up of my parents' marriage when I was five, Dad has always seemed happiest when he was as far away from his family as possible. It's not an accident that he moved to an island that is so hard to get to for so much of the year.

And now, as he lies in this hospital bed, wasted and yellow with sickness, a sickness which he has deliberately and consistently sought out, as his heart and blood and kidney functions are minutely monitored by these machines, I look at him and wonder: how can I love him, how can I save him, when I can't even *reach* him?

I NEED TO GET DAD'S PASSPORT and insurance papers from his house. For two hours I sit on a bus, travelling to his village in the north of the island. Halfway down the village street I'm spotted by a neighbour and I'm not sure how it happens but soon I have a concerned circle around me.

'Where is the English man?'

'We saw the ambulance come and take him away. Is he alive?'

The ambulance was clearly a major drama. Much of what's asked is in Greek and I can't answer. I say that he's in hospital. They cast up their hands and wail. In hospital, to them, is practically the same as dead. 'He will get out of hospital. I will take him to Ireland.' They brighten. I am waved off, with much smiling and arm patting.

I let myself into Dad's ramshackle bungalow and walk through the rooms, wondering where to find a single passport in the chaos of books and papers piled on every surface. In the bedroom there is blood all over the bed and floor, and blood and other fluids cover the bathroom floor, sink and toilet, crusty and stinking. I'm shocked. I know that I have to do something, to clean it all up, but it is beyond me. Through friends I get in contact with an ex-army couple living in a nearby village. When I show them the house and the state of the rooms, they don't bat an eyelid. They assure me that having cleaned up after the army, they can handle anything. They seem so capable and so solid that I give them the keys and leave them to it. When I come back a few days later, the house is spotless, as if the nightmare of blood and sickness could not have happened here.

*

19

After three weeks, Dad has stabilised, though he is still too weak to travel. My sister and I want to return to our lives. When we say it to Dad, he panics at the thought of us going, and we're both torn. My partner offers to fly out, but in the end I make the pragmatic decision to leave. I feel that Dad will be safe in the clinic's care – he feels that we are abandoning him.

Because it takes so long to get home, I have only been back for a day when I get a call summoning me once more to Corfu. Out of the blue, the clinic administrator says that Dad needs treatment at a hospital with a liver unit. And, once again, it feels like my heart is pumping pure adrenaline. I book more plane tickets, this time to bring Dad to Ireland. A friend of his helps us out, collecting the patient from the clinic and flying with him to Athens, while I go through the Dublin-Heathrow-Athens relay again. I meet them in the bar of the Athens airport hotel. Dad is wolfing down a chicken sandwich and a glass of orange juice. The sandwich is salty and the orange acidic, both of which the doctors have advised against. I'm relieved and irritated, a familiar combination of emotions. That night we share a room. Dad is only able to shuffle from the wheelchair to the bed. He bleats requests at me. I try to find the energy to be nice. I wonder to myself when it was that I became his parent.

In the morning, the airport staff are very kind, picking us up at the hotel and delivering us to the gate. The plane ride is uneventful, I watch a film and Dad sleeps. At Gatwick we wait a long time for the wheelchair and when it comes, and when I start pushing it, I realise just how big an airport it is. Dad insists on being wheeled around the terminal, peering from his seat. He wants to go into the pharmacy, but the aisles are too narrow. Instead I buy the supplies, then I manoeuvre him into the disabled toilet so he can freshen up. It's a brief, eye-opening introduction to the world of disability: people are very sympathetic, smiling at me, while treating Dad as if he were invisible.

Then Ryanair insists that he walk up the outdoor steps to the plane. He looks defeated, as this is totally impossible for him. Ryanair is adamant that he can only board if he is able to do so by himself. The stalemate finally ends when the airport staff put us on the cherry-picker lift they use for loading food deliveries. It's a short flight, but Dad is now exhausted. We arrive in Dublin and are met by my sister and her partner. We drive straight to A&E at St Vincent's Hospital. I register him at the desk, able at last to speak the right language. In the triage room, the nurse asks him questions. Then she says she wants to take some blood. She reaches for the blood-test tray. And without her really looking, or pausing in what she is doing, or even particularly noticing that she is doing it, she takes a fresh pair of gloves from the box on the wall. And I exhale. It's going to be okay, I think.

Everyone is confused when Dad is discharged from St Vincent's later that night. He is so evidently ill, and barely able to walk, that we are shocked he is not being admitted for treatment. When I appeal to his nurse, she tells us that there are beds lying empty in the liver unit, but the hospital is so understaffed they can't open them. When I complain to the A&E manager, she tells us that he's better off at home than on a trolley in a corridor. She seems blithely indifferent to the fact that he has nearly died. Or maybe she just sees it all the time. He is given an outpatient appointment to attend the liver clinic the following week.

The days out of hospital give Dad time to rest, and to eat normally again, but at the liver clinic, as we sit and wait, I realise that he is not much improved. He is hunched over, breathing shallowly, and groaning every so often. The consultant insists on seeing him alone. When Dad emerges from the office, he has a sheaf of prescriptions and a follow-up outpatient appointment for two months' time. I cannot believe that this is it, that there will be no medical treatment for a man who is so seriously ill. I ask at the desk if I can discuss it with the consultant, but I am refused.

Still, Dad dutifully takes his pills, stays off the drink, and slowly seems to regain some strength. After several weeks he is recovered enough to feel restless. Armed with his medication, and full of promises to look after himself, he goes back to Greece. Writing that statement now, I can't quite believe it myself, but he did go back. Though still far from recovered, he was desperate to be at home, among his books, and away from doctors. And away from daughters.

But predictably, within a few weeks, though he is resolutely not drinking, Dad's health is again at breaking point. He flies back to Ireland, unaccompanied this time. In the airport I barely recognise him. He is emaciated, with a hugely distended abdomen that makes him look – as he says himself, shakily – like he's having triplets. I hold his hand as he gasps for breath. We take a taxi to A&E where he is admitted, but still without a bed to go to, he is put on a trolley in a corridor. People come and go around him. The noise is constant. Even at night they don't switch off the lights in the corridor. In prison this is called 'white torture'. Though he was already in a bad state when he arrived, over the next couple of days his condition visibly deteriorates.

My sister and I go back to spending our time sitting by his bedside, badgering nurses and doctors for information, for treatment, for a bed. By the third day, Dad is hyperventilating and can barely speak. He grips the handrail of the trolley, and looks at us beseechingly. When the consultant finally appears, he refuses to address his remarks to me, demanding that I go away so he can hold his 'confidential' patient consult in the hallway. As I skulk around the corner, I count five patients within hearing distance of Dad's trolley, and countless staff and visitors. To make things even more farcical, Dad is so delirious by now that he has no idea what the consultant is saying. He is taken upstairs 'for tests'.

When Dad gets back to A&E, the registrar is kinder, explaining that the ultrasound scan shows that Dad has ascites – a build-up of fluid in his abdomen, leaking from his organs and other tissues, and putting so much pressure on his lungs that he can barely breathe. Simply put, he is at risk of drowning. Now that his case is urgent, Dad is finally admitted to the liver ward. It takes two days to drain twelve litres of fluid from his abdomen. He phones to tell me this astonishing statistic. I am in the supermarket. I think about what twelve litres looks like as I reach for a carton of milk.

The draining process stops with about five litres left to go. To drain any more might precipitate kidney failure. The procedure has been successful though – Dad's belly has shrunk and he is now able to breathe properly. Then the consultant tells him that he is on a transplant list. Dad says, 'Absolutely not.' The consultant says it's not up to Dad. Dad says, nonetheless, he would rather die. I'm shocked by his refusal. But with the fluid drained, the threat of death, which has been so ever-present over the past few months, seems to recede. I don't think he's going to die, not this time. Prescribed with strong diuretics to stop the fluid building up again, Dad is discharged.

He moves into my sister's house, but after weeks of his brooding presence, she suggests he stay with me. My partner and I live in a one-bedroom apartment, so we buy a folding bed and he sleeps in the living room. We try to get on with our lives, to go to work, to live normally, but it's impossible. This can't continue. Neil offers to help and together we talk Dad into renting a room elsewhere. He does not want to go, and he acts as if he's being sent to Siberia. I overrule him. There is a power to running someone else's life when they are not able to do it themselves. I arrange his hospital care. I book the flights. I pay the bills. I tell him what pills to take. I decide where he will live. But, in reality, it is Dad who has all the power. Because he is the one who decides if he's going to stop drinking. Or not.

As the season turns to autumn, Dad is stable enough that the doctors grant his only wish: permission to go back to Greece. He hasn't had any alcohol since he got ill, and he says he plans to stay dry. Maybe we can all return to normal. On the radio I hear reports of young men who have died from binge drinking, of an older man killed in a drunken fight. It is the death toll of a drinking culture. The list is a long one but though my father's name is not on it for now, the awareness of that inventory, increasing daily, is always with me.

WHILE DAD HAS BEEN RECOVERING, his best friend Neil, who had been such a source of strength for me, so concerned about every step of Dad's illness, is on the receiving end of a diagnosis himself. Suffering from a persistent cough, Neil goes for tests and, though outwardly active and healthy, he is diagnosed with cancer. It is terrible. The two men meet in Dublin between their various treatments, and both are shocked, I think, by the other's physical state. When Dad returns to Greece, Neil continues to phone me, weekly now, to discuss Dad's prognosis, always upbeat and encouraging, with a generosity of spirit shown by few, I imagine, who have such substantial concerns of their own.

In November the news comes that Neil's cancer is terminal, that it will be only a short time until the end. Dad flies back to Ireland, so that they can see each other once more. He is so nervous and on edge as he sets off to see Neil that my sister and I go too. We have a few moments with Neil first, and his face lights up as he tells us that he thinks Dad has rediscovered himself. 'He wants to live again.' And Neil is right: somehow facing death has pulled Dad back into life, with all its struggles. Dad spends some time with Neil, alone. We stay in the kitchen, waiting and trying to lend a bit of comfort to Neil's daughter. A week later, she rings to say that Neil died that morning, 11 December 2013. It was — it is — a great loss.

One of Neil's last wishes is for Dad to speak at his funeral. With the winter flight schedule, however, it is too short notice, and we can't get Dad to Ireland in time. Instead, he writes the eulogy and, in his absence, I read it at the crematorium. I hope, as I read, that people hear Dad's words as if they came from him, as he salutes his closest and dearest friend of forty-six years. In his eulogy, Dad describes his grief that the joy that Neil found in the world, 'a joy far greater than most of us will ever know', was taken from him, too early. He writes that the trust, respect and love he shared with Neil was something he never knew elsewhere and will never know again. After the funeral, Neil's son says to me, simply, 'They were brothers.'

In that last meeting, Neil gave Dad a map marked with places in Greece that Neil had loved and thought his friend would love too. After the funeral, Dad learns that Neil has left him a financial bequest to enable him to visit these places. Dad takes great comfort from this and starts to plan his trips. I listen to him describing these plans and I am relieved. Drinking was always Dad's coping mechanism and I have been afraid that, faced with the hardest farewell of all, he would try to find some consolation in alcohol. But, although he is distraught at the loss of his best friend, he stays sober. I like to think that this is another part of Neil's legacy.

IT IS THE FIRST ANNIVERSARY of Dad's haemorrhage. On a visit to the liver clinic in Dublin, the consultant tells him that his organ functions have significantly improved. He is no longer on the emergency transplant list. After the appointment, as we absorb the good news, I ask him how he feels about what he has gone through. He says he remembers very little. He says he thought he was dying, but when he goes on I realise that it's not that he doesn't remember, but that he actually *misremembers*. 'At least I was never in any pain,' he says. I am astonished. I insist on recounting to him how he spent one entire day roaring in agony, as three doctors clustered around his bed, and we were banished from the room, reduced to listening anxiously from the hallway. He looks sceptical, as if I'm making this up; it doesn't match his memory of the experience. This happens again and again as we talk over our different versions of this recent past, with Dad claiming not to remember any of the pain, or our interventions to save him, to care for him, to help him and us to survive the crisis. I initiated this conversation, but now I hate myself for asking.

He'll never have the memory of my sister and me trudging through the rain every morning and evening to and from the hospital and our hotel; of the long hours and the physical tension of waiting for the doctor to come; of the disappointment that there were no straightforward answers. They aren't his memories, they're mine. And so he'll never know how it felt for the two of us to sit next to his hospital bed, constantly checking his breathing, his heart monitor, his transfusion bag. Or that as I sat there, I cursed him for always acting in a way that forced us to make these sacrifices. What was the other option? That winter morning, when I woke and saw the text message that said he was bleeding, I lay in the dark for a few minutes, knowing that I would get up and respond, knowing that I'd been preparing for this moment for years, but also wondering what it would take to do *nothing*.

As he talks, I am incensed that instead of asking how we felt – perhaps through shame, perhaps through the same narcissism he has always manifested, or perhaps because he just wants to move on – Dad has chosen to remember a different version of events. In his memory, he is a stoic hero. In his memory, we figure as only occasional characters. In his memory, our feelings do not count. Perhaps I'm the narcissist here, wilfully reminding him of my presence, reinserting my sister and myself, with a word, a gesture, a story, back into his version of that time. Because his memories are not good enough for me.

He tells me that I am a bully. Maybe he's right.

IT HAS BEEN FOUR YEARS since these events. It has taken me those years to write this, to collect my emotions and gain some distance. Dad has been faster at all these tasks.

In late 2014, Dad writes a piece for the *Irish Times* on his life with alcohol, and his life afterwards. He sends it to me and my sister for our approval. One line stops me in my tracks: 'I am totally impenitent in the sense that I do not regret any of my drinking life.' Though part of me admires the honesty he shows in this declaration, I cannot let it pass. In an email, I tell him that I have problems with his characterisation of drinking. For a start, I find it strange that the piece doesn't acknowledge any of the brutal hurt inflicted during his career as an alcoholic. Later, on the phone, he says that he is taken aback by my reaction, that he didn't realise he was hurting anyone. For a man with so much time and space for self-reflection, there's pitifully little actually done. I explain it to him. 'Oh,' he says.

The next day, when Dad sends the piece to the editor, he copies me in on the correspondence, a tactic he consistently uses to include me, but also implicate me, in transactions where he feels he needs a witness. (I should point out, in case it is not already obvious, that he is adept at getting into arguments.) To the editor he says that he is anxious that his daughters will accept the piece but that one of them (that's me, then) has pointed out that a drunk father is a destructive parent. However, he says, he does not think that the piece should be a 'breast-beating apology to the world, or my daughters in particular' and so he is happy to publish the piece as is. Throughout this back and forth I can see that Dad is concerned not to hurt me or my sister. That he does not change the article in light of my objection is not, however, completely unexpected. He may have discovered a new emotional sensibility, which had been anaesthetised for decades by his drinking, but he is still himself: still self-centred, still obstinate, and still unrepentant.

The article appears in the 'Health & Living' supplement, an association that we all get a good laugh out of. He makes the newspaper's front-page banner, not quite 'my battle with drink' but not far off it. I am unsure how I feel about this. For years I have been impatient with the euphemisms for alcoholism, such as my father has 'a great fondness for a drink' or that he's 'the life and soul of the party'. Finally, here it is, a clear declaration on the front page – 'I am an alcoholic' – and I am proud of him for it and, yes, admiring of the guts it took to write it. I buy multiple copies without quite knowing what I will do with them.

But I am also angry. I am angry that the piece does not try to face the damage done to us all as individuals and as a family. I am angry that he can't see that alcohol was not his friend but his enemy. And I am angry that he chooses to focus in the article on his post-liver-failure diet restriction – no salt – which means that he can't eat out in restaurants any more. Big deal. I am angry just generally, even at the line where he calls me and my sister 'walking saints'. It is too easy to say, another bullshit euphemism. Enough. I decide I need to write my own narrative.

When I was a child and Dad was beginning to struggle with the depression that has characterised his adult life, he made me promise that, when I grew up, I would not become a writer. I solemnly said the words. But inwardly I knew that I would do the opposite. Because what my dad really taught me, despite himself perhaps, is that writing is a way of making sense of the world, a way of processing – of possessing – thought and emotion, a way of making something worthwhile out of pain. And so, inevitably, as I sat beside him in those hospital rooms in Greece, I wondered how I would describe the room, and the man in the bed, as if it, and he, were a scene. I wondered how to tell the story of blood, of nurses and gloves, of doctors and waiting. I wondered who was the protagonist, him or me. And I wondered how I would, if I could, use these notes as a way of understanding the larger story of me and my dad.

Things are better now. I no longer monitor Dad in the way that I did. I no longer even go to his hospital appointments, trusting him to talk to the doctors and manage his medication and take responsibility for his own health. I roll my eyes when he fails to take proper care of himself, when he wears light canvas shoes in the pouring rain, when he loses his bus pass, when he insists that roasted peanuts, and dried soup mixes, and even *bacon* do not contravene his no-salt diet. I roll my eyes, but I stand back. His principled stubbornness is not only unassailable, it is what guarantees his vow to never drink again. And it is more than that too. I stand back because I know that he does not need to ask my permission, he does not want my opinion, he does not belong to me. As I try not only to read him, as I have always done, but now also to write him, I see beyond my judgement of his alcoholism. I see that he is happy. One of his close friends tells me that they laugh together again, which hasn't been possible for a long time. If drink was a means for Dad to numb the pressures that can make life feel monstrous, then it was also numbing the qualities that make life joyful. Things are better now.

I finally finish this essay. I phone Dad to tell him that I have written about my memories of his health crisis. He makes a non-committal sound, then asks me to email the piece to him. After I press 'send', I sit at my desk in a fretful silence, worrying that he will be upset by what I have written. I worry that he will criticise it. I worry that he will dispute its truths. Most of all I worry that by writing it, by sending it, by hoping to publish it, I will break the fragile calm that we have built between us, in the years since he stopped drinking.

Twenty minutes later, I have my answer. He has written two short lines: 'It is beautiful. And brave.' As I parse his response, I realise that here is a moment when my father has surprised me. I thought we had lost the capacity for surprise. But we are not lost, not just yet. Our relationship may be an unyielding kind of story, a chain of unalterable moments, from arguments in bars to vigils at hospital bedsides. But it is also, just as powerfully, an ever-changing conversation between two people, father and daughter, a conversation that we are both grateful is not over. These days, sometimes he'll call and I am busy and he is self-involved and I snap and he snaps back and I hang up. I text him that I will phone later but, often, I forget my promise. Sometimes he'll call and he'll tell me his news, some village gossip that I can barely follow but I listen anyway, and when I yawn he laughs and I laugh too. Sometimes he'll call and I don't feel like talking. Sometimes he'll call and it is just so good to hear his voice.

And every time he calls, my heart races. My heart will always race.

FROM THE
BABY YEARS

I PEE ON STICKS and into sample cups. I pee on my own hand when the stream won't obey. I open my legs wide for sex, for the doctor's speculum. I hold my arm out for needles and blood pressure monitors and sometimes to grasp onto my partner as he sits next to me. I am fearful and hopeful and shameful. I worry that I am empty, or that I am full of the wrong things. I worry that I am disappearing, eroding, failing. I do not know what to do with all these feelings. I only want to be a mother. Why is that so easy for some people and so hard for others? Why is it so hard for me?

The question was always difficult. Do I want kids? I agonised for years. I tried to stage it as a debate, with pros and cons. I weighed freedom against love, selfishness against selflessness, presence against legacy. In my twenties and early thirties, I watched as my friends answered the question with a 'yes' and became parents. I saw the shock on their faces, the tiredness in their eyes, the extraordinary range of emotions provoked by the new person they had made. And I saw the love.

I was not alone in this agonising negotiation: my partner, R, felt the same. Together we talked about the possibilities of becoming parents, together we talked, almost nostalgically, about our lives as people who loved quiet, and calm, and the space to read and write. On the page those may seem like little virtues, but that list represented for me, for us, a peaceful, happy, fulfilling life. A child would mean giving all that up for years. Would it be worth it? I was anxious that I would re-enact my parents' mistakes, anxious for my relationship, anxious that, confronted with a small, crying person whose needs I would have to meet, I would feel it was an impossible task. It felt like a blind choice between what I had and what I might have. It felt like I was risking everything. And I did not know that it would be worth it.

I MEET SOME FRIENDS in a park one Saturday morning and we sit and talk and drink our take-away coffees and watch their children playing on slides and swings and that thing that spins round and round. One of the kids falls off. There is soft bark underfoot and the child is not harmed, but, shaken, she runs over to her mother, buries her head in her lap, looking for a cuddle. And there it is. The love. My stomach churns and I have to stand to disguise my sudden influx of emotions. Releasing her mother, the child sees me standing there, and she takes my hand. She guides me to the swing-set and I lift her up and start to swing her and she laughs and smiles, all shock forgotten. And there it is again, the love. The love undoes me and all my protests about peace and quiet and calm. I want this love.

For a while I keep this epiphany to myself, afraid that it will not be shared by R. When I do tell him that my mind is made up, he is still hesitant, and there are some slow and difficult months during which we talk and don't talk about this huge thing that I think I want to do and that he thinks he does not want to do. A baby is not something I can make on my own, despite what I've heard from friends who secretly stopped taking the pill so they could get 'accidentally' pregnant. I cannot imitate their acts of simultaneous faith and betrayal. I want to make a family with this man, the best person I know, the person I love the most. I want to go through this with him, to share the love.

One evening, a moment comes. I arrive home from work. It's raining and I'm soaked and R meets me at the door, takes my dripping coat, and asks me if I'm alright. I'm miserable, and it's not because of the rain. I can't help myself, I start to cry. 'I'm just so sad. All the time. I want a baby of my own.' He is equally upset. He tells me he'll do anything, anything at all, just to stop me from being this kind of sad. I say again that I want to have a baby. He asks me if I'm sure. I say yes. R isn't sure, but he's now unsure enough to allow me to sway him. 'Okay,' he says.

THE FIRST TIME we have unprotected sex it is *weird*. We try to pretend that it is not weird. We get used to it. We both imagine that if we have a lot of sex then pregnancy will follow. But the fun and games of having sex all the time pall a bit as the months go by and I start to wonder why sperm and egg are being so coy at this whole getting together thing.

Then, eight months into *trying*, as they say, I am late. I only notice this belatedly, while I am in another city at a conference. I check into my hotel and, as I'm unpacking, I curse myself for not remembering to bring tampons.

Then I realise that I should have got my period already. Huh. I leave the hotel. Like some sort of secret agent, I walk in the opposite direction to the conference, trying to find a pharmacy where I won't bump into another delegate. I buy a test and stash it in my bag as I head back towards the venue, sweating slightly. At the opening reception I stand amidst circulating trays of canapés and warm white wine, but all I can think of is how soon I can excuse myself and make for the toilets. I sit in a narrow stall for what feels like an age, and then with trembling hands I unwrap the test. I read the instructions, I pee on the stick and I wait. Women come and go, flushing and washing. I don't let myself look until the minute hand tells me I've waited long enough. It's faint, but there is a positive line. Holy shit. What have I done? I leave the reception. At the hotel, I do another test, and it's positive again so, with wildly beating heart, I dial R. While I am freaking out, he sounds calm, if physically far away. He reassures me and as I listen to his voice I start to believe we can do this. Still, I spend a restless night plagued by the fear that I have just lost control over my life.

The next morning I give my paper, and I don't even bat an eyelid when the PowerPoint doesn't work, because secretly I'm wondering what the hell I'm even doing here. But when I do a third test – because, well,

I'm needy like that – it's negative. I don't understand. How can two tests yesterday be positive but one test today be negative? I get on the phone again to relay this new news, and a still-calm boyfriend tells me it'll be fine either way. I make it through the day and spend another sleepless night at the hotel. The next morning, I invent a kidney infection and abandon the conference to go home.

R goes with me to the late night surgery, and the doctor does a few tests, just to be sure, but they're all negative and he tells us it was probably a 'lost pregnancy'. He takes some blood, suggests that I relax, and that the next time will be for real. A bit shell-shocked by the barrage of conflicting information over the past forty-eight hours, we head to a friend's birthday party, and order tall beers, neither of us sure whether we're celebrating a reprieve or drowning our sorrows. The next day, post-adrenaline rush, we are both subdued. And we are both disappointed. I realise what I'm feeling is grief. R says he feels the same. We both really want to be parents, and it's time to stop leaving it to chance.

I head for the pharmacy, buying half their stock of ovulation test kits, trying to ignore the annoying picture of a grinning baby on the box, hoping I don't see anyone I know, and wondering how I became the person who buys these things. As soon as I get home I crack open the packet to start tracking my cycle and to discover my 'optimum conception days'. I read and re-read the instructions. I can't believe there are only three high-fertility days per month. Three? I remember back to the panic we were made to feel as thirteen-year-old school-girls in the annual compulsory sex education class. We were *terrorised* with the idea of getting pregnant, made to feel that if a penis waved anywhere near our vaginas we would get knocked up. But now that I want to get pregnant it's magically revealed to me that the baby-window is fucking *tiny*.

I start the process of tracking my cycle and I go through all the phases, from eagerness to boredom to resentment. Though I'm monitoring myself, I reject the enforced jollity of online fertility calendars that animate each month with images of cherubic babies and hearts. Likewise, I shudder at the fertility manual's helpful tips on getting my partner to observe my physical 'signs'. *Get him to tell you when you seem premenstrual.* Well, we're not doing that. And perhaps that's because I'm a little embarrassed myself by some of the requirements.

I read that my cervical mucus is meant to be like egg-white for optimum sperm motility. Right. Before now, I didn't even register that I had cervical mucus, but now

I've got to become a connoisseur of its consistency. I make an omelette just to remind myself what egg-white looks like. And then I move on to probing my own body, inserting a finger, and, following the instructions in the manual, stretching the fluid out, recording my observations. Some days it is thick and white, some days it slithers oleaginously. These are the good days. I write it all into my diary, next to the schedule of classes I'm teaching. Cryptic signs allude to no mucus, too much mucus, *perfect mucus*. And when it comes to announcing to R that today is the top day for implantation, I find out that what I've read is true: waving a recently-peed-on ovulation test stick at a man as an invitation to sex is not, actually, sexy.

The ridiculousness of this behaviour has to be acknowledged; in fact laughing at the absurdity of it all seems like the only sane response. Doing ovulation tests when you're at work, between teaching classes on European avant-garde theatre, and trying to remember not to pee for four hours so that the reading can be accurate – if you haven't tried it, let me tell you, it's both ludicrous and stressful. Unfortunately my default way of dealing with stress (pouring it all out to friends over a glass of wine) isn't an option at the moment, given that for half of each month I'm keeping my fingers crossed that I'm pregnant. And when I mention the unsexy ovulation-stick moment to a friend, one of those friends with three kids who got pregnant 'without even really trying', she pats me on the arm, pityingly. I solemnly resolve in that moment never to share bodily-fluid stories with my fertile friends. I quickly come to realise that infertility is a particular kind of loneliness.

Though most people don't know that we're 'trying' (oh, how I begin to hate that word), the friends who do know offer mixed advice, ranging from the best sexual positions for conception, to the problems of a tilted uterus (but how do you know if you have one of those?), to the joke that drunk sex, or – astonishingly – sex while on drugs, will definitely result in pregnancy. I am so paranoid about why I'm not conceiving, and fearful that I'm doing it wrong, that one night I get deliberately drunk before launching myself at R, on the off-chance that they're right. Another friend shocks me when she blithely says that I should consider adopting a child as she knows several couples who conceived naturally once they 'got into adoption'. She cannot be serious, I think. I move the conversation to another topic.

In search of more like-minded companionship, I go online. Pregnancy message boards are new to me and I find myself haunting them, yearning to find an answer through my screen. I get to know the acronyms, which are, in their own way, useful, bizarre and a little bit sad. When they don't want to say 'sex', they say BD (baby dance); when they don't want to say 'fail', they say BFN (big fat negative); and when they daren't say what we're all really hoping for, they say BFP (big fat positive). I am moved when women post long messages about their infertility, their slowly expiring hopes, and the ways they beat themselves up for failing. I am moved when I read the comments on these posts, in which women cheer each other on, in which women give each other support, in which women point out that none of us is failing.

The months wear on until it's more than a year since we decided a baby would be a good thing. I'm still not pregnant. My GP tells me to relax, and then to relax some more. She suggests that I try to stop thinking about it, because obviously thinking about it is what's causing sperm and eggs to disobey the biological imperative. As advice, this seems perilously close to asserting that women's minds are dangerous to their bodies. I make an appointment with a different GP. But when I ask her what my options are, she says, sadly, that it's IVF or nothing, and 'that's very expensive'. She offers to print off the 'Getting Pregnant' help sheet from the NHS website. I tell her, thanks, I'm good for print-outs.

***

AND THEN I'M PREGNANT.

On the way back from the doctor's office (I'm taking no chances this time on home tests), R and I can't stop grinning. He takes me by the arm and looks me in the eye. I see that he's both crying and smiling, as he says he has thought about it and he knows what it would mean to me and he wonders if the baby could have my last name. It is a precious, joyful moment. I have long speculated (aloud) why children automatically have their father's names. R's suggestion means, to both of us, that we may be changing our lives but we won't change who we are. The same week as the pregnancy is confirmed we go 'Sale Agreed' on a house. A house that's big enough for a family of three.

But, very soon, there is blood. And it is every morning. Tiny amounts, yes, but enough to make me worry. 'Relax,' says the nurse. 'It's probably old blood,' says the doctor. I want to believe them but my fear makes me look at the internet. I search online for 'bleeding while pregnant' as I wait to meet a friend, then again as I wait to catch a bus, and again as I stand in the supermarket, basket on the ground, in the pasta aisle. Because it shouldn't be every day. Because it's very red to be 'old'. Because the internet tells me it's an early sign of miscarriage. I go back to the pregnancy message boards. They allow me, on the one hand, to believe it's going to be fine, and on the other they confirm my inner voice, which says it's not. I'm not alone, that's for sure, there are a million messages posted out there, and I read both happy and unhappy outcomes. I follow certain stories that sound like mine, and when a thread goes silent I ache to know why. Are they too busy being pregnant or too sad to post? I thought I'd be done with the anxiety by now, but instead of relaxing, I have shifted from wanting to be pregnant to needing to be still-pregnant.

It's such early days in the pregnancy that barely anyone but us knows. I haven't even told my father, as he is caught up in his own medical drama, post-liver failure. I find myself in normal conversations, with friends and colleagues, or just in random meetings, wanting to scream out loud the fact of my pregnancy. I need to share the symptoms, the little proofs (my jeans are definitely tighter), the reassuring truths (those two little lines), and the side effects (I am constantly light-headed as my body manufactures new blood in preparation). I feel it like a pressure building behind my lips, caught in my throat. One night in a stuffy theatre foyer, I faint. A sympathetic friend offers me a brandy. He's only trying to be nice but I leave, muttering an angry excuse. The fainting makes me even more afraid, and the next morning, still in bed, I phone Holles Street maternity hospital. I tell them about the previous lost pregnancy and that

I'm bleeding every morning. The woman on the phone says I should come to the drop-in clinic where I'll get to talk to a midwife. It'll mean the morning off work, and a couple of hours sitting in a queue, but I start to feel calmer.

This is, of course, the moment when I kick myself for not having private health insurance, the kind that comes with access to doctor helplines and scheduled appointments. Why, oh why don't I have it? My mother advised me to take it out, my friends talked about the benefits of different packages. I visited friends and their babies in their semi-private rooms, and heard them talk about their consultant visits. All paid for by health insurance. But me? Nope, I got none. Idiot.

In the waiting room everyone else looks like they've had practice, and I'm the only one without a bump. I tick the box for 'advanced maternal age' (aka 'geriatric', the official medical term for new mothers over thirty-five). We have both brought books, and R actually seems able to read, but mostly I pass the time gazing at the other women and the posters tacked up on every wall, many on smoking and pregnancy, or the benefits of breastfeeding, others with helpline numbers for women experiencing domestic abuse. When I'm called, we go through to a cubicle and I explain my history to the doctor (midwives are scarce today it turns out). The ultrasound machine is brought over to the bed, and now we get to do the bit I've seen on TV. After a few anxious moments of pressing the sensor into my gelled abdomen, the doctor finds the foetus, clearly defined, and where it's meant to be. Phew. But then she says that the machine is too old, so she can't get a good enough image. Can I come back for a follow-up appointment in the foetal clinic? She prints off the picture of my uterus with the white blob that means 'baby'. When I take it, I see that I'm shaking.

The second appointment is a few days later and together we wait in a corridor. As we're waiting, the Master of the Hospital walks past, tidies some sheets on a trolley next to us, and, as an afterthought asks if we're being looked after. I recognise her from the news. I say yes we're fine, though I want to say that the Victorian skirting boards look grimy. In the Foetal Assessment Unit, the doctor from downstairs is here again, with another, senior doctor, who, it transpires, works for the same university as me. I have a moment of hoping this coincidence will make her well-disposed towards me, as if her liking me will make a difference. The scan this time involves an internal ultrasound. I pretend like I've done this before, as I follow instructions to take off my jeans and underwear and to lie with my feet together and knees falling apart. I wonder what R is thinking as he sits next to the bed. A plastic probe, covered in latex and lubricant, is inserted into me to see the hidden uterine landscape. It is not painful, but it is uncomfortable, and I am horribly aware, suddenly, that my body is no longer private, no longer knowable to me. My body is, as I experience it, red and fleshy, soft and warm. But on the screen there's just a grainy greyscale, like a lunar landscape. The monitor is angled away from me, but even if I could see it properly, I wouldn't know what I was looking at.

The examination is conducted in silence. At the end, they remove the probe, wipe it off, discard the condom, then give me a paper towel to wipe myself. Quietly they ask me about conception dates – could I have got it wrong? No, I couldn't. I know not only the date, I know the encounter, the white sheets on the bed, the closed blinds, the light still on in the bathroom. I remember the tense conversation that preceded it when I asked if we could try tonight, and I remember when I said no, it wasn't okay with me if he was 'tired'. I remember it because we did have sex though he didn't really want to, going through with it only to avoid my sighing cold shoulder. I remember it because it was the moment that I became an emotional bully. I remember it because when I saw the positive sign on the test, I felt that it had been worth it.

'Yes, I have the date right,' I say.

The doctor looks sad. 'Let's hope then.'

Oh no. No no no no no no.

Maybe I am wrong.

Maybe the date is wrong.

Let me count.

Let me see a calendar.

Let me rearrange the timeline.

As we leave the hospital, R says that he doesn't know what's been implied. I say I think they meant I'm having a miscarriage. He says that they told us to hope, so that's what he's going to do. I shake my head.

Seven days later, exhausted and numb with worry, we are back at the hospital. In the cubicle I am told to get ready for another internal ultrasound. I take my jeans off, lie back, feel the cold probe. Hope. But there is no heartbeat. After a few moments of silence, the midwife leaves to get a second opinion. The second midwife measures the foetus onscreen. 'There's been growth,' she says. Following this statement the two women tell us that they '*Can't say anything or any more.*' What, what can't they say? There is an insane moment where both women look at the floor, and the second-opinion midwife repeats it, 'We can't say anything. You'll have to come back in a week.' They leave the room.

I need to pause, I need to reason this through. Growth means life. But no heartbeat means no life. It is only with a great degree of hindsight that I think I understand. There is no life, but somehow there is growth, and growth means ambiguity. In Ireland, the equal status of the foetus and the mother in the constitution represents more than simply a ban on abortion. It means that in the case of any ambiguity, the life of the foetus is prioritised; and in our situation it means that it is illegal for the midwives to pronounce the pregnancy over. Ambiguity does not mean that there will be a baby. Instead, it means the total disempowerment of us as 'parents' of this ambiguous pregnancy. The midwives' silence, though it is completely uninterpretable to us in the moment, actually speaks volumes. They can't say, and we can't know. I am furious. At the situation and, specifically, at them. I am a woman, in grief, and these women will not look me in the eye *as a fellow woman* and tell me that I'm not going to be a mother. It is quite something to find myself in the National Maternity Hospital, not only distraught at the end of a wanted pregnancy, but denied the right to know what's happening inside my own body.

We leave the hospital again and walk, stunned, in the

direction of home. We're both torn between rage and paralysis. Another week is just too long to wait. But what can we do? That evening, in desperation, I book an ultrasound appointment with a private clinic. It's expensive, but – fuck it – maybe rich people get better treatment, better answers. Two days later we are in the waiting room and it is like another world, with plush carpets and soft drinks while you wait. But we're the same edgy, needy people. I wonder will we get any different response here. When the midwife comes to collect us, our hope for an answer expands. She has an English accent.

In the room, in the moment when she turns on the ultrasound machine, the image of a perfect *in utero* foetus appears onscreen. I flush with the wild hope that this perfect recognisable *baby* has somehow transposed itself into me, but it's just the residue of the last appointment, and as she moves the probe, the screen goes blank and it's back to grainy moon surfaces and R holds my hand as we go through it all again. There is no heartbeat today either. The midwife turns back to her desk and writes some figures on a chart. I speak into the silence. I say that we need to know. The midwife hesitates. She says that legally she can't say anything. And then she pauses. In her experience, she says, she has never seen a foetus at ten weeks develop a heartbeat. It's the 'No' that I've feared and expected and I hate hearing it. I hate hearing it. But I'm almost elated to at last be given the answer.

I don't remember much from the days that follow, beyond a vague recollection of our shared despondency. I think we went to work, I think we saw family, I think we tried to pretend that we were okay.

Five days later we are back in the hospital for our last scan. This time there's no growth, no ambiguity. We cry in the hallway, then we're taken to a private room. It's small and narrow with a couch at one end. I sit down but there isn't quite enough room for both of us, so R stands. He looks at a pile of leaflets on the side, and says, 'I think we're in the bereavement room.' With the weird giddiness of grief, we start to laugh. Of course this is the moment that the surgeon chooses to come in and I can't help thinking that he'll judge us, will think that we're not devastated at all and that, maybe, our miscarriage is just as well. Or maybe he's seen everything in here. Either way, I'm not laughing now. The surgeon explains that I have had a 'missed miscarriage'. Since my body is holding on to the foetus, I need to have a surgical procedure to remove it. Everything is very different now that there's no baby and I'm back to being the primary patient. Suddenly, I'm the one that matters.

On October 18th I am admitted for what they call an ERPC. It's another terrible acronym; this one translates as 'the evacuation of retained products of conception'.

The original doctor, from the first appointment, comes to my bedside to do bloods and check my stats. She has paperwork and she asks me, as 'the mother', to sign a form for the disposal of the foetal remains. This catches me out. I cry. The nurse sends me a counsellor. She gives me a folder on coping with miscarriage and I tuck my first ultrasound printout into the back. And then it moves swiftly: I'm taken to the operating theatre, I'm back on the ward, I'm being discharged. My mum picks us up. The rush-hour traffic is at a standstill. R nearly loses it, frustrated by the delay, by the day, by absolutely every single fucking thing. I realise that no one is minding him because he's expected to be the strong one.

I take a week off work, my boss is understanding. My family are supportive. My sister calls my dad to tell him, and then he phones me, his voice solemn with concern. At the weekend, we have lunch with R's family, studiously avoiding any mention of what this week has really meant. When the conversation turns to the house we've just bought – the house with the extra bedroom that I so want to fill – I get upset. R's dad hugs me and R takes me home. No one else knows. Though the miscarriage is the only thing on my mind, and I feel like I'm falling apart, I don't talk about it. I don't even want to talk about it. It's too raw, and it's too hard, and it's too shameful. And, besides, since no one else has ever talked about, or even mentioned, their miscarriage to me, I believe I should be mute too.

TWO MONTHS LATER, when I go back to the hospital for a follow-up consultation, I walk past a row of huddled, smoking women, heavily pregnant, their bellies barely covered by their dressing gowns. How is that fair? I silently demand. I would be a better mother. I deserve it more. I try to push these terrible thoughts away, but a visceral jealousy courses through me. At the consult, I ask about physical post-miscarriage symptoms. I say that my period has not returned and the nurse says that's normal. I say that my body feels different, and she gives me a compassionate look, but says nothing. After I leave the hospital I go and buy some new bras, in a smaller size, angry that my breasts, which should be buoyant with pregnancy hormones, have become smaller, as if my body, like my fertility, is shrinking.

It takes months for blood to return. And my bleeding, once so regular, is now so rare and so scanty that I barely recognise these abbreviated episodes as periods at all. I am always told that I look young for my age. But I feel the opposite, as if I have internally aged, as if my sluggish, broken, failed uterus is poisoning me from the inside out. As if I'm barren. It's hard to argue away this feeling, a dejection that settles and suffocates. I drag myself through, rather than out of, the torpor.

The one person I confide in is the GP, until she starts talking about 'Mother Nature' and how I need to 'let nature take its course'. This seems inestimably stupid to me and I retort that no one thinks it's a good idea to let nature take its course when someone has cancer. I am so deep into this that I don't even see the problem with comparing not being pregnant to a serious illness. I say that I am drowning, not waving, and I need help. The GP agrees, reluctantly, to run some tests. As the (pregnant) practice nurse takes my bloods, she suggests a mindfulness course for 'inner peace'. I snort. But when she says that she knows women who have conceived after acupuncture, I start to listen seriously. I decide to check acupuncture out – it's expensive but I can claim some of it back on my new and exorbitant health insurance plan. I phone the number she gives me.

As so often with semi-alternative therapies, the interview with the acupuncturist feels as healing as the treatment itself promises to be. His consultation room is in a basement, its walls festooned with pictures of babies. I sit in a comfy chair and he asks me about my physical and emotional state. As usual, I feel weird describing the bodily minutiae of it all, but he nods at everything I say. Finally he asks me if I'm easily distracted. I say no. He looks sceptical. He tries again. Do I do multiple things at once? 'Oh, yes,' I say. He tells me then that I am typical of someone with too much busyness and not enough quiet, too much yang and not enough yin. Usually, I react badly to being told I'm overdoing it – a mantra not just of GPs but of my family, and friends, and colleagues – but I am here for an answer, and it helps that he frames everything within an ancient tradition of understanding the body, because isn't that what I've been trying to do this whole time? Understand my body?

And so begin ten weeks of lying on his couch, trying (despite myself) to be more meditative as scores of fine needles rebalance my energies. He also has me taking massive doses of spirulina, a gagging green powder that I can tolerate only (at my sister's advice) mixed with blackcurrant squash. 'Come on,' I think as I glug it down. 'Come on,' I think as I lock my bicycle to the railings outside his office. 'Come on,' I think, 'let me make a baby.'

But I don't get pregnant and my fertility signs – blood and mucus – don't improve. Disheartened at the lack of change, as I pay for the final scheduled session, I feel my faith in this endeavour ebbing. I should continue, he says, and I sense the unspoken verdict in the air, that I am an extreme case, irretrievably unbalanced. Maybe if I were more easy-going. More placid. More, well, more maternal, all cuddly and warm. Maybe if I were completely different, if I could swap out every cell, and gene, and chromosome in my body, maybe then this would work. In the early hours of the morning, unable to find sleep, I realise that what I'm trying to be cured of is being me. Maybe my late thirties is the age to admit I'm never going to change my personality, or my body. Because I may not be pregnant, but I don't hate myself, even with my too-much-yang nature. I like that I have ten things on the go, all at once. I like that I'm always planning for the next thing. I like that I bring a high energy to my life, that I see it as a challenge. I like that my favourite thing to do on the flight home is to look at the airline route map to pick my next destination. But then I remember the baby photos, and all the 'thank you for getting me pregnant' cards on his shelves. In the morning I text the acupuncturist to wish him Happy Christmas and to say I'll see him in the new year.

I host Christmas for the first time. R's family joins us, and there's my mum, and my sister and her partner. And there is an unborn member of the family. My sister, V, is nearly nine months pregnant.

She told me in May. We stood in my kitchen, as I made tea, and she was nervous and I reacted badly. I should have thrown my arms around her in celebration, but I only managed a forced 'congratulations'. I am ashamed of this reaction, embarrassed that I could not, for one moment, shed my narcissism. I felt cheated. And I felt every one of the five years that separate my older body from her younger one. It took me a full twenty-four hours before I felt any joy for her.

Seeing my pained reaction, V decided not to talk to me about her pregnancy and not to show me her ultrasound scans. I didn't even realise, I didn't even ask, until my dad bragged that he had the latest *in utero* shot printed out and fixed to the side of his computer monitor, where he could keep a constant eye on the next generation. I begged her to send them to me too, to include me. She had an early scare when she, horribly like me, had some bleeding. But her emergency scan showed a healthy foetus. As her pregnancy developed, and her bump grew, we all gravitated towards her. It has long been the case that while I try to manage everyone in the family, V is the one we all turn to for care. Feeling bad? V will listen, say the right thing, and serve you homemade cake with your favourite kind of tea. I sometimes think that without her we would all just drift apart. Whereas I am usually off, being busy elsewhere, she is here, she is home.

Christmas goes well. We pull crackers. We eat too much. We load up the dishwasher.

THEN ON DECEMBER 30TH my mum calls to say that V is in the maternity hospital and that she needs company; her partner is at work and can't be reached. She's only at thirty-seven weeks, so I figure that the baby is making an early appearance. At the registration desk they have no record of V being in labour. I phone her. She texts back that she's in the Foetal Unit. On the fifth

64

floor, I give V's name to the two staff at the nurses' station. They exchange a look, a look that means bad news. But I have no idea of the scale of the badness.

I am led around the corner to a private room. There's a bed and an ultrasound machine. There's a chair in the corner, where V is sitting. She holds her bump. She is sobbing. She tells me in gasps that her daughter's heart has stopped.

I hold her and hold her and wish for the world to go away, for time to stop, for the words to be unsaid. In total disbelief I look at the midwife, who looks embarrassed. Soon my mother is there and V's partner is on his way. He phones to ask where we are and I meet him at the top of the stairs. 'What's going on?' he asks me. I stop and tell him and he runs to the room, takes V in his arms, shuts the door. We wait in the corridor. The nurse offers to bring my sister tea. I insist that she doesn't like tea, as if that matters today. After a while, V and her partner emerge. She reassures us that she's okay and they want to go home.

Two days later we are back in the hospital for the birth. There are four of us in an overheated room off the main maternity ward. V is in the bed, and her partner, my mother and I are arranged on chairs, trying not to watch her, as we all wait for the drugs to begin her labour. They give her the full dose of painkillers and, when her contractions start, the maximum epidural. As the nurse explains, nothing can possibly harm the baby now. V and her partner are taken to the delivery room, Mum and I wait some more. Mum wants to talk, she cries and I pat her back but I don't want her to cry, because then I'll have to cry, and I cannot cry because I have built a wall of steel around my heart and I need it to keep standing.

Late that night, Elena Jane is born. It is New Year's Day, 2015. Baby daughter, beloved grandchild, adored niece.

Mum and I are allowed into the delivery suite. V is lying propped up, holding her daughter, who is swaddled in the blue cotton blanket all newborns are wrapped in. V looks up at me and smiles. I say, 'Beautiful baby girl,' not sure who I mean, my sister or her child. We hold V as she holds Elena. Elena looks perfect, only impossibly still, and there's a tiny little rip on her eyelid, with a little blood, where her delicate skin was damaged during her birth. When I take her, her compact little body is too light, but she's warm, still holding the heat of her mother's body.

It is so quiet in that room as we stand around the delivery bed. Remember this. This is the only time you will ever hold your niece. This is the moment when she is the closest she will ever be, out in this cold world, to being alive. This is the end and the beginning. Remember this.

V asks me to take photographs of her and Elena. She smiles and offers her beautiful child for the camera. I do not know where she finds the strength. The next week I have the photos developed at one of those print-your-own shops. I'm inept with the machine and the manager comes over to help. He tells me his own son was still-born two years ago. He doesn't charge for the prints. I have copies made for all Elena's close relatives. When I send them to my dad, he protests, 'How could you? How can you look at them?' Because V managed to smile, I tell him, as she held her daughter. All you have to do is look.

In the days after Elena's birth, we all need something to fill the time. Mum cleans every room in her house. V and her partner drive around Dublin, try to pack away the baby things, drink coffee at Mum's house. We hug each other. We talk about funeral arrangements. We rarely make eye contact for fear of the tears we'll see. And for me, suddenly, after twenty-three years of vege-tarianism, I have a deep craving for meat. I see no reason to resist it. In the time between Elena's death, her birth and, ten days later, her funeral, I eat everything in my path.

And I shop. I shop for the house renovations that we have finally started. I pick out bathroom fittings and tiles. The January showrooms are surreal places. I have to leave the first one, my flood of tears startling the shop assistant who had asked me what kind of bath we wanted. At the second, I just point at the simplest, cheapest models. I shake my head when asked to choose between mixer taps. I look at the shiny chrome and I wonder why this is what I have chosen to do on the day that Elena is lying in the hospital mortuary, the place they call the 'angels' room'.

On the day of the funeral, I go to see Elena one last time, to sit with her in the hushed room at the funeral parlour, to tell her that I love her and that I will look after her mummy. At the chapel, I watch my sister's shoulders. She holds them straight. I have never seen anything more heroic.

The time with Elena was so fleeting. V was pregnant for nine months and knew her daughter, her movements and rhythms. For each of the rest of us, we watched from the outside as V grew large with her, felt her kicks. Even for Elena's father, this was the limit of knowing her before she was born. And with so little to remember, I find myself deliberately playing and replaying my few memories. It annoys me that though my impressions of the days around her birth are incredibly vivid, I forget small details, the order of things, the exact time she was born. After her funeral, I find myself telling strangers about her, I install her picture on my phone, I call her by her name, all just to keep hold of her. Since Elena's presence in this world was so delicate, so fragile, I love her extra fiercely, asserting and re-asserting her existence. Even now, I think of her every day and wish, every day, that it was different. I don't want to celebrate her in her absence, or to hold her in my heart; I want to hold her in my arms, laughing or crying, but not, not as I held her in that delivery room, so beautiful and so soulful, but so unquestionably, so irrevocably gone.

Milestones come and go. Relentlessly. V's due date. One month since Elena's death. One month since the funeral. We spend the first Mother's Day together. V makes a rainbow cake. Then comes the autopsy results, showing no underlying genetic problem, just a tragic heart anomaly. V's partner starts to raise money for the National Children's Hospital, to support the Heart Unit and the children for whom there is still the hope of treatment. We all wonder if there was any way that Elena could have survived. What if we'd known? Could some intervention have changed the outcome? My colleagues donate the proceeds from a charity lunch and cake sale to the fundraising project. V's partner and his friend do a parachute jump. V and I do the Women's Mini-Marathon. Before the race, we all get together to hand over the cheque to the representative from the hospital. We're in a crowded hotel basement function room.

People mill around in groups, branded with t-shirts bearing the names of different diseases. Every person has a story, a child whose survival, or whose memory, compels them to be there. It is a way of doing something when there's nothing to be done.

Very soon, V's maternity leave is over. But soon too, with joy, relief and nervousness, she tells us that she's pregnant again. This is a pregnancy that goes well, that doesn't have a sad ending, that results in nine months' time in a healthy baby boy. This is the pregnancy that she should have had the first time around. It's bitter-sweet. It's hard. It's healing.

INSPIRED BY MY SISTER'S COURAGE, I decide that I need to know what is wrong with me. We register at a fertility clinic. I start a series of tests and examinations to find out more about my reproductive system, convinced there must be an identifiable reason for not conceiving. The consultant says male infertility is easier to deal with, and so I actually feel disappointed when R's sperm count comes back normal. It must be me. But test after test shows there's nothing actually wrong with me either. I go for weekly internal ultrasounds, horribly accustomed by now to the probe, and hopeful each time that some non-compliant part of my uterus will reveal itself. I am ovulating, which seems to be the holy grail, though my uterine lining is thin. The fertility drugs will boost this, I'm told, but I'm not reassured, because no one can answer why my period cycle is nowhere near what it used to be pre-miscarriage. Why is it that no one but me seems that bothered by this? I have pages and pages of daily charts of my ovulation, discharge and bleeding. I show these charts to every doctor that I see, and every single time the doctor smiles patronisingly, barely glancing at the top sheet, before shoving the charts in the back of the folder.

Still, I persist. In late summer, I'm in Holles Street Hospital again. God, I hate this place. This time I'm in for an exploratory procedure. As usual, I'm naked from the waist down, lying on a plastic-covered reclining chair, feet in stirrups. My fertility consultant is here, and two nurses. There's another internal probe, but this one has a camera at the end of a long tube that sprays warm water. The water will clear any blockages and the camera will see what's going on with my fallopian tubes and ovaries. It is painful from the beginning and it gets worse as the camera moves further inside me. I start by asking questions but soon I cannot speak. I am so afraid of betraying myself by crying out that I deny even to myself how painful it is. The nurse sees my clenched face and gives me her hand. I crush it.

When it is over, the consultant tells me that women often compare the pain of this procedure to childbirth. She calls me a hero and suggests I take a couple of ibuprofen. And then she tells me that there are no blockages, no unhealthy lining, no dodgy tubes. I should be pleased, but I realise I wanted there to be something concretely wrong with me. I stand to go, still leaking water. 'Was there anything else today, Emilie?' the doctor asks. There is so much else. Fix me, I want to say.

But maybe I can't be fixed. When we go back to the fertility clinic the consultant says that since I was last tested, at thirty-six, my egg reserve count has depleted significantly. She likens the reduction of fertility to falling off a cliff. She says that the decrease makes IVF urgent. 'Don't wait,' she says. 'Don't wait even six months.' As soon as she says the words, I nod because I'm ready to do IVF, to sign the papers, to go through it all for what I want. I treat it as if it were a straightforward decision. But then I remember to ask about the process. We listen as she explains the injections, the medication, and the egg-harvesting procedures. Did I mention that I hate injections? Having seen me get bloods taken, R shudders at the expectation that he'll administer the shots. He asks what the likelihood of multiple births is. We've heard of more than one couple with IVF twins. The consultant smiles and says there's minimal chance of that happening. It seems an insufficient answer.

To lighten the mood, I think, she remarks that after all the injections, all the petri-dishes, and all the lab-fertilising of eggs they 'throw them in and hope something sticks'. *Throw them in*. The casualness of this pronouncement makes me feel like throwing something myself. Despite the tests and the internal probes, from where I'm sitting, and the lack of answers I have been given, these people seem to know next to nothing about what actually makes a pregnancy work.

I ask about the odds of conceiving. She says 28%. In the days after the consultation I do a little further research. With my age and egg reserve, it's more like 20%. I'm confused, again, by the lack of transparency and the absence of answers. Read the other way, it's an 80% likelihood of not getting pregnant. If it were a case of paying this clinic the €9,000 they quote us and getting a baby at the end I'd be there like a shot, brandishing my chequebook, no matter how many injections and how much stress the hormones caused. But the odds are bad, and it's a lot to pay, and I don't know how much more disappointment I can take. In the foyer of the fertility clinic, we look at each other. I say that we can raise enough money for one round of IVF and I vow that I'll stop at that. But R looks sceptical, because he knows me better, and we both know that I hate to fail, and so if it doesn't work the first time, I'll beg and borrow for a second cycle at least. Let's talk about it, he says.

We end up in the park across the street, though it's threatening rain. The seemingly ever-present bulk of the hospital is visible through the trees, so we pick a bench facing away from it. We sit a little, and wait, knowing that the words we say will be crucial. And we have what is probably the most important conversation of our lives. He says the odds are terrible, and I give him that. He says that the process looks to be miserable, and I concede that too. He says the whole thing is making him unhappy. Me too, I say. But, I add, being unhappy now makes me more determined to grit my teeth, in the hope of a better future. He says it makes him question the whole thing. He points out that we've been bickering lately. A lot. I open my mouth to contradict him, but yeah, we have. Still, I say, it'll be worth it in the end. And then there's silence.

I knew that sex on demand had not been great for our intimate life, but I hadn't realised that we were so far apart. For months I'd been feeling lonely; it didn't occur to me that he might feel the same. I had ignored and shut out his objections, impatient with his hesitancy about IVF and seeing his oppositions as another frustrating example of the 'leave it to Mother Nature' dogma. I was terse when he pointed out that I'm not sick, and that it's good news that there isn't anything actually wrong with me. I'm broken, I countered. Look at me. Un-pregnant equals broken. When I elected to go for the painful and invasive tests, he was sympathetic but simultaneously reluctant. I snapped at him that I was making all the effort.

We have both wanted a baby and we have both tried so hard and we have both felt the heartbreak of miscarriage. And now we both have to face something else: the reality, and the emotions, of perhaps not becoming parents. We sit on the park bench and I feel sad and lost, but he takes my hand, and I listen. I listen as he suggests that we remember our lives are about more than infertility.

My close friends who have tried IVF have not been successful. My best friend underwent several cycles unsuccessfully. She and her husband are now divorcing. I have watched other friends go through similar anguish. On the other side, I also know parents who have had children after miscarriage, and parents who have happy endings, wrung from multiple fertility clinics and multiple rounds of treatment. And we know people who have managed to adopt, though that in itself was a gruelling, years-long process. I am torn between recognising the hardship that fertility treatment puts couples through, and believing that if I just try a bit harder then I could be a mum.

But I can no longer avoid the fear that I will lose what I have in the pursuit of what I may never have. If things continue as they are, then there may be no baby, and there may be no relationship either. We agree to pause. This means more than not going ahead with IVF. Not 'no sex', but 'no sex to a fertility schedule'. We're going back to normal. It's now late September and we decide to return to the conversation in four months.

And instantly things improve. I sleep better. We're nicer to each other. The bickering evaporates. It's like we have been set free. Really. It was amazing to me then, and it still is. A friend once advised me, as we watched his toddler daughter learning to walk, to just make a decision. Either do it, or don't do it, he said, but don't lose yourself in the limbo of maybe doing it. Now, I understand the wisdom of this. Making a decision is incredibly empowering. Following our park bench conversation, I occasionally catch R looking at me, checking to see if I am really okay or just pretending. Having done it my way for so long, now we're trying it his, and I see him taking responsibility for my happiness. But stopping really does come as a liberation to me too. Because, finally, I can stop obsessing about my body. I can stop noticing what movement of my cycle I am in. I can stop the charting, the monitoring, the *peeing on sticks*. And I can comprehend how oppressive it has become. And I can relax.

The relief for all of us through all these months is that V's second pregnancy is going really well. It is not without its stresses, and it is an act of pure faith for them as parents to risk it so soon, but the baby is healthy. In comparison, my own baby-thoughts feel minor. And soon it is January again, the first anniversary of Elena's death, and her first birthday party. Though we celebrate her life with a birthday cake, New Year's Day will never, now, feel like a moment of renewal, but only a reminder of her loss.

In mid-January R and I look at each other. It's a long look, a charged look, a look tender with mutual compassion. It's a look that confirms it: no IVF.

IT CAN BE DIFFICULT to leave the 'trying' behind. As we attempt to get back to how we used to be and to begin to accept that maybe there will be no baby for us, there are moments that challenge my resolve. One day I decide to tackle the leftover ovulation tests and baby-making books that hide in the bottom of the wardrobe. It's a bit of a watershed, to throw these all away, and I'm dismayed by the pile of plastic. I can't see any markings on the packets so I phone my sister to ask if she thinks they're recyclable. She hears the panic in my voice. 'Oh, Emilie,' she says sympathetically. 'Just throw them in the bin.'

The decision not to undergo IVF was not lightly made. Talking about 'fertility' is a bit like when you're a kid (or a university lecturer) and you learn a new word and, suddenly, you see and hear it *all the time*. Everywhere we turned there were reminders. Once we'd realised conception wasn't happening easily, it seemed as if there were ads for fertility clinics on every radio station. Newspapers carried full-page ads, one with the slogan 'Everything you thought you knew about fertility is wrong'. This particular ad runs, literally, for years. At the time of writing, it's *still* running, still getting scrunched up by me as I shove it in the recycling bin. The coincidences go on. My favourite podcast includes a segment on relationships that broke up because one half of the couple didn't want children. I read a great film review and when I check the author's byline I see that she has written a book on her decision not to have children.

And despite one in six couples having trouble conceiving it feels like everywhere, everyone has kids. That work peer I decided must do nothing but work, as she zooms ahead in her career, has twins. That conference keynote speaker? Two books and two children. Do either of these women ever sleep? Or sit down? Or finish a cup of tea? Sometimes it feels like we're all still competing at that worn-out game, 'having it all'. Only, of course, I don't. Pregnant bellies spring out at me. People's social media pictures show not only their bumps but the proudly smiling co-parent too. I scan so many profiles looking for that rare thing – a happy couple without kids – that I feel a surge when I catch a re-run of *Sex and the City* and hear Carrie asserting the value of a life without kids. Has it come to this, life lessons from a fictional shoe addict?

Other things have shifted too. A younger colleague, who definitely wants kids, asks me if I think she should wait to get pregnant till her second book is done. Unhesitatingly, I say, 'Don't wait.' Am I telling her to lean out? This is not how I would have responded a few years ago, but she and her husband really want a baby, she has tenure, so go for it, I say. Take the time. In fact, looking at my own record (as I belatedly apply for promotion), I realise that the year after my miscarriage, I published nothing. I worked really hard, I set up a research network and spoke at conferences, and taught students and marked endless exams. But I didn't write.

In fact, I abandoned the draft of a book I'd been working on, a draft I still haven't gone back to. That gap in my life, the wasted baby years on my CV, goes unexplained. How do I ever reflect, on paper, the grief that stopped me in my tracks?

It's hard when people ask me, as they regularly do, if I have children. They mean well, though it's a terrible question to ask a woman in her late thirties. Because there's really no easy answer. Occasionally I'm tempted to look around and say, 'Oh yeah, I *knew* I forgot to do something.' But I can't bring myself to make such a false joke. One evening I go out with a friend and, after too many glasses of wine, she earnestly informs me that it is my fault I'm childless, that I shouldn't have left it so late. The remark cuts through me and I have no response except to get my coat and go home.

AT THIRTY-SEVEN WEEKS, my sister goes into labour. I visit the hospital to keep her company with doughnuts and funny stories. There is a heart trace monitor for the baby, and we eye it warily, but it is so different this time. Still, she and her partner are jittery, and V is particularly stressed when her labour stretches on for two days.

Finally, late on the second night, my nephew is born. I am at home, waiting up, annoyed that I can't be with her for this birth, when my phone beeps with a message from her partner. It is a photo of the baby, his wrinkly face and bunched-up hands so different from, and so much like, his sister's.

At the registration desk the next morning they try to tell me that visiting hours have not yet begun. I dodge past them, because the rules don't apply in this moment, and nothing is keeping me from my sister and my nephew. They are in the last room on the corridor, and pushing open the door, I see that she is fine, and smiling, and holding her son. She passes him to me, a wriggly little warm bundle. Welcome to the world, little one.

I AM NEVER GOING TO HAVE A BABY. I am anxious about this fact. And I am grieving. And I am happy.

One persistent anxiety is that I never understood why it wouldn't happen for us. For all the research and testing – mine and the medical profession's – I still don't know what went 'wrong' with my body. Why is that? As I consider this question and I look back on those months and years and our trying and our failing and our appointments and our second appointments and on and on, a pattern emerges. A pattern in which I am not taken seriously, or we are not taken seriously. Or not seriously enough.

I feel short-changed. Not just because I couldn't have a baby, though that looms large. But because of those weeks when we were denied the right to information on our foetus. And because, after the miscarriage, time and again, I met the attitude that as a woman I'm only the one who feels, not the one who thinks, not the one who should have access to information, not the one who should be empowered to control her own body.

There are days I think I could have – should have – tried harder to exert that control myself. I should have followed a gluten- and dairy-free diet, given acupuncture more time, gone to more than one fertility clinic. Although I know, deep down, that I gave it everything, I still find ways to beat myself up. What I never thought I'd say, because I thought it was clichéd bullshit, is that I have accepted my physical inability to have children. And I'm not really the accepting type (in fact, most of the time, I don't even like people who are). Perhaps full acceptance is still a few steps down the road, because when I see my partner holding someone else's child, or, actually, when I see any man carrying any baby, I am hit with the realisation that I still grieve for my life as a mother. But the truth, what I *have* accepted, is this: I can try to have a baby and I can fail every month and be unhappy. Or I can not-try to have a baby and not-fail every month. The total number of children I have had remains the same either way, a big fat zero. But the outcome is totally different. I choose to be happy. This happiness is not perfect, or pain-free. It carries grief within it. It is all the stronger for that.

And, hurrah, at last, for forty. It was always my cut-off age. If I don't have kids by forty, I'd say to myself, I'll stop trying. Of course, I'd said that back in the heady days of thirty-five, when forty seemed far away and I'd imagined not just one but two kids filling those years. And I know that there are mums who are only just starting at forty and I wish them luck, joy and a baby that sleeps. But I'm done, and I'm more than a little relieved about it. Because now that I'm here, and I've been up and down the rollercoaster, being forty feels like a positive boundary. I can give myself permission to be someone else, someone other than a mother. Someone other than the woman manically checking her cervical mucus.

Nowadays one of the highlights of my week is Thursday afternoon, when I pick my nephew up from crèche. He laughs and plays and shouts and pushes away his bottle but eats his fruit purée. He loves books (chewing them mostly), and all shiny things, and he hates wearing socks. He has just learned to wave. The first time he waved back to me, I nearly exploded with sudden joy. I am, you see, very warm and cuddly, despite what you may have heard. I smile and wave and he smiles and waves. And there it is. The love.

ONE DAY LAST YEAR I came home from work to find R raking leaves in the garden. He smiled and I noticed in the bright autumn light the new strands of silver at his temples. And it hit me. We are growing old together. This is what it will be like as we watch each other age, as our partnership ages. And this unexpected moment made me happier than I could have imagined. I see a life ahead for us, a shared life. A great life.

It is difficult to translate a great love, a great life, into words on a page. It sounds so prosaic – raking leaves, smiling at each other in understanding – but it is in the everyday moments that the tenacity of love, and its depth, are often revealed. Though we do not have the joy of biological children, there are many ways to have a childful life. And, it turns out, there are many ways to enjoy a child*free* life, a recent, and important, shift of emphasis for me. I am done marking myself through absence. I am done using the word 'failure' about my body. I am done living and writing that story.

This is the moment that we get to look around, find our own balance, and enjoy the view from where we are.

SPEAKING /
NOT SPEAKING

MY PARENTS SEPARATED when I was five and my sister was a baby.

I remember them before the split. I remember them as a happy couple. I remember family birthdays, laughing and blowing out the candles. Them hugging. Hide-and-seek in the overgrown garden. I remember climbing up the scaffolding at the back of the house and getting stuck, and calling for help, and them both being there, guiding me down. I remember rain falling through the roof and thinking it was an adventure to find buckets to catch the water. I remember my sister being born. Toys arriving at the house for her and not for me. I remember my mum breaking her wrist when she slipped on ice. My dad sleeping in the other room.

It was winter and he made me a hot-water bottle and when I said I didn't want it, he threw it at me and it burst as it hit the wall. I remember them telling me they were splitting up. I cheered and said 'no more fighting'.

I remember moving house. My mum unpacked our things in an upstairs bedroom, because that was the only room with a proper floor. I remember it raining outside and us all in bed together for warmth. I remember my sister's cough, which lasted for months, and the walls always being damp. I remember the nice man in the local shop who let us have bread and milk on credit till payday. I remember sunny afternoons and having painting parties and the day when my mum put up a swing in the garden. I remember going to see my dad on weekend afternoons. He made us toasted sandwiches in a machine that only worked if you stood on it and you knew it was ready when your foot got too hot. I remember when his house was taken because he couldn't pay the bills and then he had no house. I remember going with my mum to visit her friends, who were also his friends, and seeing my dad's furniture there. I remember pointing and saying, 'That's our table.' I remember asking Mum why Dad's stuff was in their house and she was angry and she couldn't speak and she drove us home.

My mum drove us everywhere. She drove us to school. To the supermarket. To the park. She drove us to see Dad on weekends. She drove us to see him the time when he was in the hospital. The hospital was far out of the city centre and while she drove we sang along to our favourite mix tape. As we got out of the car, Mum warned us that Dad might not be in a very good mood. I did not understand when she said he was 'drying out'. I gave Dad a poster from my bedroom that said 'Don't Worry Be Happy'. In the years after their separation, being happy did not seem something that either of my parents was very good at.

And what do they remember? Out of all the experiences, what have they held on to? How did my mum face raising two small children in a house with no heating and damp walls and not enough money? How did my dad inhabit the space left by his family? How was it to have a husband, a wife, a marriage and then not? How was it to lie next to someone and then not? How was it to be two and then not? To be not even one, but a half of a broken two?

MOST OTHER FAMILIES did not look like ours. It was a time when people stayed together for the sake of the children, for the sake of the family, for the sake of the institution of marriage. When my parents, in typically bizarre fashion, threw a 'splitting up' party to announce the end of their relationship, one of their friends kneeled down on the hall floor and begged them to stay together. And even if a couple did separate, they were still connected, still tied, still married. There was no other choice. Because Ireland had a constitutional ban on divorce.

A year or so after my parents' split, when my teacher handed out our school reports at the end of the school term – a brown envelope for each pupil – there was none for me. She asked me to stay behind. When the other children had cleared out in a noisy rush, I approached her desk, frightened at the idea that I had done something wrong. She handed me two brown envelopes, one for each parent. Perhaps she had thought it would shame me to receive them in front of my classmates. They were all standing outside the door, though. 'Why'd she keep you behind?' they wanted to know.

I tried to make up for being the odd one out by telling stories. I did not realise that stories had to be true; I thought they only had to be interesting. I told stories to the kids in my class. I told them that I could breathe, like a mermaid, underwater. I told them that one weekend I had had a kidney transplant. I told them that the snails on the schoolyard wall were poisonous and planted there by spies who wanted to kill children.

My audience listened and then they laughed and then they called me a liar. After that, I became suspect. One Saturday afternoon I was in the kitchen at home when the phone rang. When I answered, all I heard was giggling. It was the girls in my class who had called to tell me they were having a party and that I was not invited.

Following their separation, my parents initially saw each other regularly, and had a relatively civil relationship. But at some point at the end of their first year apart, they stopped speaking. Actually, my dad stopped speaking to my mum. And so Mum, faced with little choice, stopped speaking to him too.

What is it like when your parents don't speak? I don't mean when they're just in a bad mood and not speaking to each other *temporarily*. I mean when they never exchange a word with the other. What is that like?

When your parents don't speak, you become their go-between. When you want to see your dad, you have to arrange dates and places and times to visit him. When your dad gives you a letter for 'that bitch', you have to give it to your mum. When your mum takes the letter and cries, you blame yourself. When you do something wrong and your mum tells you in her meanest voice that you're just like your dad, you blame yourself again. When your dad gets a girlfriend and cancels seeing you, you're confused. When your dad says that he's bored by children and you can go to hell, you're even more confused. When sometimes it's not your dad, but your mum who is drunk and can't drive you home or give you dinner or put you to bed, your world starts to fall apart because she's the only thing holding it together. That's what it's like.

And this is also what it's like: you're ten and your mum is out at a party and the phone rings and it's your dad, and he says that he is going to kill himself that night, and you say, 'But I love you, Dad,' and he says he knows, that you're the only person who does, and then he hangs up. And you sit holding the phone because you don't know if he means it, and you don't know what he's asking of you, but you do know that something is being asked, and you are afraid that if you don't find the answer you will never see your dad again. And then you hang the phone up because you don't know where he lives and you don't know his phone number there, and you're only ten, so you go back to bed and you cry yourself to sleep. And the next day you find his work phone number and you dial it and he answers and he is alive but now he is shouting at you for disturbing him. So you don't say anything about the night before and you don't tell your mum and you never tell anyone, because there is no way of telling this story that can make it okay.

Recently, in a box of old photos, I found a postcard from me to my mum. It is written in my large, careful, child-ish handwriting, though the address is in my father's hasty scrawl. The postcard reads: 'Dear Mummy, the weather is quite good. How are you. I hope you are well. did you know I was coming home on Monday 5th August I write just to make sure you do Love Emily'. The postcard is a lasting reminder that we were children in the days before mobile phones, before every house even had a landline phone. Still, it seems strange to me now that my dad asked his daughter to write a postcard to confirm the date when he could give us back. And then, of course, there are all the things the postcard does not say. Above her address, my dad has written only my mum's initial and her surname, as if he could not bring himself to write her full name. In my note, I don't com-ment on the postcard's image – a picture of a sailboat lost in mist – though it seems to speak pathetic volumes. And I have not written 'wish you were here'. But looking at the card now, I can see that that's what it really says.

***

WHEN I WAS EIGHTEEN, and in my first term at university, there was a referendum on divorce. One of the college debating societies put forward the motion: 'This House Would Grant the Right to Divorce in Ireland.' I went along, thinking I might learn something.

The debate played out as a kind of brightly lit theatre, the back and forth as predictable as if it were actually scripted. The arguments were well-made, well-rehearsed, but I'd heard it all before and none of it felt true to me. And when I looked at the full line-up of speakers, I realised why. Not one of the debaters represented my experience, not one of them said, 'I've been through this. Let me tell you.' It was all just hypothetical. And so they did not know what I knew. Or they knew, but did not think it worth saying. Because in all the blather about sacred vows no one was naming the real danger: the limbo of non-existence.

Apart from a separation agreement, in which my dad was meant to share joint custody, the end of my parents' marriage was completely unlegislated. Our family did not exist. And because we did not exist, we could not be protected. In real terms, this meant that my father could not be forced to pay regular child maintenance. Oh, there was the occasional cheque, but week by week, our household got by exclusively on what Mum earned.

What my mother spent on raising two children, my father spent on drinking.

As a child, I had told story after story about my parents, intoning them to myself and anyone who would listen, as a way of staving off the threat of non-existence. I had told these stories loudly and insistently because I sensed, even at five years old, that the world would rather I remained quiet, that our family was not appropriate subject matter. But even as I told them, I knew that stories could never be enough. Because stories can't make your parents talk to each other. And stories can't stop the bullies. And stories can't transform the damp, or the cold, or the lack of food in the fridge.

It was the first referendum I had ever voted in. With the capacious free time of a student, I set the whole day aside. But walking to the polling station took only fifteen minutes, and putting my X next to 'Yes', folding my ballot and posting it in the box, took only a few more. I walked out onto the street, unsure of what to do now. The tree-lined road was quiet. Nobody seemed to know, yet, the difference that had been made. I trembled but the world was still.

The next night, for some reason, I ended up at my dad's house, watching the referendum results with him and his girlfriend (both of them married, of course, to other people). Dad passed out early, but she and I stayed up, getting steadily drunker, yet still alert with the edge of adrenaline as we monitored every nuance of the television coverage. When a recount was ordered by the anti-divorce campaign, resulting in *more* votes for the Yes side, we crowed with triumph. We were not normally allies – far from it – but on this night we both saw a chance for our lives to change.

The bill to make divorce legal passed by 50.28%. With a turnout of 62.15% this means that the referendum was carried by 9,114 votes. It was a hard and narrowly won victory. The first divorce in Ireland was granted on 17 January 1997. The new rules stipulated that you had to be separated for three years before you could petition a court for divorce. My parents had been separated since 1982. Fifteen years: five divorces of time.

I remember standing in the centre of Dublin one afternoon that spring. I was twenty. I stopped on a busy pavement as people pushed past me. A sign in the window of a travel agent's had caught my eye: 'Package Holiday Deal: 1 Parent + 2 Kids'. It's ridiculous, but I was actually moved by this, an ad for a sun holiday. It was the first time I had ever seen my family reflected publicly. One parent plus two children. That was us. We existed.

WHEN I WAS IN MY MID-TWENTIES, I began to meet my dad for an afternoon pint once a week. We met in the same pub every time, sat at the same place at the bar, exchanged the same words with the barman and, often, each other. Sitting on a bar stool next to my dad, I felt a strange mixture of being both a grown-up and a child. Though he could be sulkily reticent, I usually found a way to draw him out, with talk of books or plays, our common language. Then one afternoon, with a tremor in his voice, my dad asked me if I would ask my mum for a divorce.

Still the go-between, I waited until the weekend to bring it up with Mum. I told her that Dad had a serious question for her. There was no easy way to say it: would she divorce him? My mum was making tea, and paused with the kettle hovering mid-air over the pot. My sister, sitting at the table, froze. Then they both started laughing. After a brief moment, I joined in. It was absurd, after all. That I had been chosen to relay the question, that after two decades of separation my father thought he needed to ask, and, most of all, that he actually thought she might say no. My mother's laughter subsided. Putting on a grave voice she said, 'Tell your father I'm still hoping for a reconciliation.' We laughed so hard, I bent double with the pain. The following week I met Dad. I told him Mum would grant him a divorce. 'Oh,' he said.

And then?

Nothing.

My dad had asked for the divorce because he wanted to get remarried. But it was wishful thinking on his part, and he and his girlfriend split up soon after his request to my mum. None of us should have been surprised. Dad had been spending months living by himself, first in the west of Ireland and then in Greece. With the engagement over, he made the move to Greece permanent. The divorce seemed to slip everyone's mind. Perhaps it's hard to remember that you're married when you live in different countries.

My mum's solicitor got spooked a few years ago. He worried that my dad might still be eligible to make some claim on her property. It fell to me to ask Dad to sign a new separation agreement. He agreed and then asked me to come with him for moral support. In the office, as Dad signed his name with a borrowed pen, the solicitor looked at me and asked, 'Why can't they just get divorced like normal people?'

I have no idea, really, why my parents have not got divorced. I doubt there is one, discoverable reason, much like there was no one reason that their marriage broke up. At the time of writing, my parents are still married. And they would now qualify for twelve divorces.

THE STORY OF MY PARENTS changed in January 2013 when they began to speak to each other again. It was grief that finally ended the silence, the grief that poured out when my sister's baby daughter died. My dad flew to Ireland for the funeral. I told him that if he wanted to attend the wake he would have to acknowledge and speak to my mother. I told him that he would have to be nice. He said, 'I am partly human, you know, Emilie.'

I worried that the reunion between my parents would be both stressful and distracting on the day of the funeral itself, so my sister and I arranged a rehearsal for the night before, in the foyer of Dad's hotel. It was a brief encounter. Dad looked at the ground as Mum reached out to shake his hand. My sister rolled her eyes as Dad belatedly took Mum's hand and said, 'Nice to meet you.' It was surreally funny and not funny at all. When it was over, I walked Mum to her car. She said she was shocked by how much he'd changed. She said she did not recognise his voice, but then again, it was so long since she had heard it. Later that evening, my sister told me that as Mum and I left the room, Dad had turned to her and asked, 'Are you sure that was your mother?'

The next day, at my sister's house, Mum and Dad sat and talked. I think they consoled each other. They were both, after all, not just parents, but grandparents now. Though it was radical for me to see my parents having a conversation after so many years, it was revolutionary for my sister. I watched her as she watched them. She had been a baby when they split. Now she was a mother, standing at her daughter's wake, seeing her parents talk for the first time in her life. Afterwards, I asked my mum what they had spoken about. She said that Dad had told her about his liver failure, and his feelings about stopping drinking. She said that they had spoken of the death of a mutual friend. And then she said that the day, and the decades apart, had given her a licence to finally talk to him about the miscarriage they had suffered themselves. I couldn't believe it when she said that they had never spoken of it before. I realised in that moment that there had been layers of silence within their marriage, and not just at its end.

My parents broke their silence because of a family tragedy. To their credit, in the years since then, they have not reverted to muteness. In fact, they speak regularly, by phone and email, and even meet for coffee during Dad's visits to Ireland. It is good news, good for all of us, their chatting and texting and being able to be in the same room. It makes everything so much easier. But it is not all happy families. Sometimes my mum phones me to tell me about the latest annoying thing my father has done or said. She repeats the phrase 'your father' while listing his faults. 'He's *your* husband,' I angrily remind her.

My anger at having to learn and respond to the new parental status quo takes me by surprise. I realise that I never expected them to speak to each other again, and so I never expected to have to deal with my emotional reaction to them speaking. And the emotions only seem to multiply. I am amazed. I am hopeful. I am relieved. I am confused. I am resentful. I am angry. And I am, unexpectedly, *aghast*. How is it that all those years of silence can simply end? How is it that all the hurt and pain and bitterness can dissolve away to nothing? How is it that we were made to endure so much acrimony for so long? And how is it, why is it, that no one has ever said sorry to me or my sister? The story may have changed, but part of me is still five years old.

It is embarrassing to admit to my inner child. I feel like a kid throwing a tantrum, stamping my foot and demanding that my parents pay attention. I am especially embarrassed when I look around and realise that other people do not seem as burdened by their upbringing as I am. Having divorced parents has become so normal that it seems overdramatic to label my parents' estrangement as exceptionally disturbing. In the absence of any particular trauma that I can point to, I can only suppose that I felt – feel – the minor pains of childhood more than I should.

WHEN I LEFT HOME AT TWENTY, I could sense my life opening, and a new separation beginning. On the shelves of the kitchen in my student flat, I piled up two saucepans and one frying pan. I stacked two plates and two bowls. I laid out four forks and two knives and four spoons. A chopping board and two mugs completed the set-up. I looked at all this equipment and I felt both ready and completely unprepared for what came next. Life beyond my parents. I wanted that life and yet was also terrified of it. I wanted the freedom of feelings that did not involve them, though I was also overwhelmed by the shape and scale of those feelings. Who was I, really, without the defining boundary of my family? What stories would I tell now?

My parents separated when I was five and my sister was a baby. Though I am a long way from the difficulties of my childhood, I still dwell on the stories of those years, hoping that they might explain the troubling residues of so many feelings and thoughts and actions. My parents did not speak. My father suffered from depression. I was a lonesome child. Those facts, and all the accompanying stories, whirl around. I write them down. Perhaps they will be less overbearing that way, pinned in one place.

As I step away from the page, and I look at what I have written about myself and my family, this family, our family, I see that in the end it is always going to be both a complicated and a simple story. In this story, which I may never stop telling, I try to remember what it was like for me as a child, and what I did and what I could have done differently. I try to imagine what it was like for my parents, and what they did and what they could have done differently. I remember us happy, and I remember us sad. I remember us divided and I remember us together. I remember everything, and I remember only fragments of a whole that will always be beyond me.

NOTES ON BLEEDING
& OTHER CRIMES

FAMOUSLY, THE TRICK TO GOOD WRITING is bleeding onto the page. I picture the male writer who coined this phrase, sitting at his typewriter, the blank sheet before him. What kind of blood did he imagine? Blood from a vein in his arm? Or a leg? Perhaps a head wound? Presumably it was not blood from a cervix. I have so much of this blood, this period blood, this pregnancy blood, this miscarriage blood, this not-pregnant-again blood, this perimenopausal blood. It just keeps coming and I just keep soaking it up. Stuffing bleached cotton into my vagina to stem the flow, padding my underwear, sticking on the night pads 'with wings', hoping not to leak on some man's sheets, or rip off too much pubic hair with the extra-secure adhesive strips. Covering up with 'period pants', those unloved dingy underwear choices pulled out from the back of the drawer every month. And all along, I was wrong, I should have been sitting down at my desk and spilling it across the page, a shocking red to fill the white.

I WAS AT SCHOOL when I got my first period and I was mortified. It was geography class and when we stood up at the bell my friend leaned over and told me that the back of my dress was wet. I looked at him in surprise, assuming he was joking. But when I glanced behind me, I saw that he was right – there was a patch of dark on my skirt, and a small pool of blood on the plastic chair. My classmates, seeing my embarrassment, stood back silently to let me pass. In the girls' toilets I sat hunched and resentful, wadding toilet roll to protect me for the rest of the day. I did not want it, any of it, this blood. At home I rinsed my knickers at the bathroom sink, hung them to dry at the back of the airing cupboard, and hoped no one would notice. Unable to bring myself to have the dreaded *becoming a woman* conversation with my mother, I shoplifted tampons and tried not to cry when it burned as I put one in, my whole body clenched against the process. Wipe, insert, pad. At twelve I felt a lifetime of bleeding ahead of me. And I felt my body had let me down.

I had never been good at noticing the passing of time. There were moments I even forgot what day it was, but now I had an internal calendar that I could not ignore. The relentless monthly bleed. Wipe, insert, pad. In my refusal to adjust to this new rhythm, there were times I got caught out. Once I was on holiday and, too late, realised I had packed no sanitary protection. I tightly bunched the hotel's toilet paper into a rough tampon, winding more again around the gusset of my under-pants. I went to the bathroom frequently to check for leaks. When, a few days later, the bleeding stopped, I cried with relief. Other girls seemed equally ignorant about the realities of bleeding. In my school, a myth circulated that your vagina would somehow seal itself upon contact with water, even during your period. I disproved this during the after-school swimming club. Luckily, the pool was crowded with girls so no one could identify me as the culprit who had turned the water cloudy with her blood. On another occasion, my period started one night at a friend's house. I woke up in her spare bed, hot with cramps, and wet between my legs. When I realised I had stained her sheets, I wished for the earth to open up and swallow me.

I was unbelievably squeamish about blood. Not the sight, or feeling, or smell of it – but the saying of it. 'I've got my period.' Where did I learn that these were shameful words? I can't have made this phobia up all by myself. Maybe it was in school when we – the girls, that is – were sent to 'Education for Living' classes (the boys simply vanished – to extra sports, it turned out). Though notionally about periods and pregnancy, 'Education for Living', we learned, was about using hand cream (not too much), and wearing the right size bra (not too small), and the right length skirt (not too short). About how to apply foundation, and when to shave your legs. About eating an orange in segments, like a lady. When a girl asked, perfectly reasonably, what we should do if we got our period in the middle of class and had to ask to go to the bathroom, the instructor said, 'Tell your teacher that you're *menstruating*.' She placed great emphasis on the last word. We stared at her.

Blood is dirt. Isn't that what the label 'feminine hygiene' tells us? Sanitary products for our unsanitary bodies. In fact, period blood is so dirty that it must never be shown. Instead, ads for tampons and towels demonstrate their absorbency with a bright blue liquid, poured cleanly out of a laboratory beaker. As a teenager, I did not recognise this sterile-looking fluid as like anything that had ever come out of my body. But then, I wasn't meant to – that was the point. My body, and its blood, were taboo. I'm not sure it's so much better now that tampon and towel companies advertise their products with uplifting rock songs and clear-skinned smiling teenagers. They may look different, with their emphasis on having fun! and celebrating! and adventuring! all while having your period. But whether it's compact tampons for teens or maxi-pads for grown-ups, somehow the blood is still invisible. And so the message remains the same: blood is unknowable, blood is unshowable.

As an adult I still find it hard to say I have my period. Even within feminist conversations some aspects of bleeding can be taboo. There is a current slogan that makes me laugh: a woman can do anything a man can do, and do it while bleeding. But at the same time as laughing, I'm also wondering – what if I can't? Sometimes my hormones flood me, then leave me high and, literally, dry. Sometimes I am doubled up in pain. Sometimes even the idea of standing for any length of time leaves me feeling faint. I do not feel like a feminist hero in these moments, I feel like I want to go home and get back into bed. But in a world where women are still over-identified with their bodies, where women have to prove their intellectual ability over and over, what is the threshold for claiming this pain? If you have a headache, it's strain from too much thinking (I'm so brainy, I'm so busy). If you have a sore back, it's from over-exertion (I'm so fit, I'm so active). A stress attack? (I'm so hard-working, I'm so important.) But a cramped abdomen? (I'm so female.) It's unspeakable.

Blood is never more taboo than when you're naked. There are men who are into menstruation, who desire sex with a woman who's already wet, who want to lose – or is it get? – their 'red wings'. But I remember only too well the first time a man saw my period blood and it is not a happy memory. We were in our twenties, and we liked each other, and he was cool and I wanted him to think I was cool. And we were kissing and then we were fooling around and then we were having sex and then he looked down. Seeing blood, he pulled out of me, and suddenly there was blood everywhere – blood on my inner thighs, blood on the sheets, blood on his penis. And he screamed like he thought he was dying. Actually dying. And I thought that maybe I was also dying. Of shame. That was the first, but not the last time I found that a man could want to share all kinds of bodily fluids with me, but not blood. Another time a man said he was 'fine with it' but got me out of bed as soon as he had come so he could wash the sheets. Another time – at the mere mention of my period – my chivalrous date phoned me a taxi to take me home.

In my twenties I liked having sex during my period because I knew I could not get pregnant. In my thirties I stopped liking it for the same reason. Over the years that I was trying to conceive, I became afraid of the appearance of blood. In my new obsession with 'my menstrual cycle', which translated month by month into 'my not-getting-pregnant cycle', I scanned my body for signs: bloating, a jab of pain at the point of ovulation, the rope of clear cervical mucus that meant I could conceive, the pink smear in my underwear that meant I had not. The blood became a curse, one that I could not shake and, as the months stretched into years, I truly began to hate this blood. No longer just inconvenient, it left a new kind of stain: infertility. People talk about making peace with difficult life events, but what do you do if the event you're trying to come to terms with is happening inside your own body? I was back to not being able to talk about blood, not being able to say it to my boyfriend, relying on him to intuit it, because to say 'I'm bleeding' was beyond me. I went shopping instead, I figured that if I couldn't have a baby, I could at least have a new dress. And every time I looked at my credit card statement, I would note wryly that here it was at last: my menstrual cycle, written down in numbers if not words.

For three decades I have lived within a silence that declares periods too embarrassing, too unwanted, too *female* to talk about out loud. I have done this for so long that I almost no longer notice it. Almost. But now I am sick of the silence and the secrecy and the warped idea that blood is taboo when it comes out of a vagina. Because it is *just not fucking good enough*. To hell with covering up, with being embarrassed, with being silent. For most of my life I have had a monthly period. For most of my life I have smiled through PMT and heavy flows and cramps. And for most of my life bleeding has been painful, physically and emotionally. And so for the rest of my life I will not be silent about it. I will talk it, write it, spill it. Blood will not just be my ink, it will be my subject.

I have a body that bleeds. Once a month it squelches, wet and hot, with blood. This blood runs out of the side of the pad, it stains the crotch of my jeans, it drips onto the bathroom floor when I forget to replace the tampon. It is inconvenient and messy and necessary and vibrant and drenching and awe-inspiring. And it is *red*. And it is *loud*. And it is *mine*.

***

OR, RATHER, IT WAS. If I felt shame at the onset of bleeding, those feelings are multiplied ten times over at its ending. I am filled with dread as I check my body, inserting a finger into my dry vagina to feel if there's blood coming, in a parody of my teenage fear of pregnancy. Let there be blood. Lots of blood.

What do other women do when confronted with the ways their bodies change? My internal monologue used to complain about luxury tax on tampons, but now I'm nostalgic for those pubic-hair-ripping night pads. Of course, it's not sanitary products that I'm really mourning. The gradual shift towards menopause – which started in my late thirties – is an incontrovertible sign that my body's childbearing years are almost over. The fact that there was no actual childbearing (can you *bear* a miscarriage?) makes this an even greater loss. One I need to find a way to articulate.

When a friend mentions her menopausal symptoms, she half apologises. 'No, keep talking,' I say. I'm so grateful to her for saying it matter-of-factly – cramps, sweats, smelly discharge. Because I'm discovering that the greatest social embarrassment is not the one concerning periods, but the one that muffles and obscures the unproductive female body. We know the debates about HRT (or do we all just know there is a debate?), we know about hot flashes and night sweats, and we concede that maybe there's a bonus to contraception-free sex. What is not said, or what I'm not hearing being said, is what it feels like. How the absence of blood feels. How your body starts surprising you. How what was wet is now dry. How what was vivid red is now brown or gone entirely. How it smells *different*. How it smells *old*.

And what are my symptoms? Orgasms can now give me cramps that could floor an elephant. My breasts look less . . . perky. I am too hot all the time. Except, of course, when I am too cold. PMT is worse, not better. There are days I experience what can only be called despair. And my bleeding is rare, unpredictable, unrecognisable. I get the occasional heavy day, a series of blood clots, a viscous, ferrous, tarry substance I can almost roll between finger and thumb. I look at this *old blood* on the toilet paper before I flush it away. This is my body. But it feels alien. I have to learn it all over again. I have to learn to be a woman who does not bleed.

One night last summer I had an argument with a friend who said we were middle-aged. He wore it as a badge of honour. 'I'm not middle-aged,' I said to him, over and over. Why did I defend this position so passionately? Perhaps because the signs that I am no longer young are unavoidable. Perhaps because the label 'middle-aged' was, for him, just a phrase, not an actual bodily change. Perhaps because if getting my period was 'becoming a woman', I fear that the end of my period is the end of being a woman.

AND THIS MAKES ME THINK AGAIN about what part of me – not just the rhythm of my life, but actually me, who I am – is constituted by my body. What does my body say about me? And what do I say about my body? I ask these questions of myself as if they can point the way forward as my body changes, as I accept that I am middle-aged, as I think about what being a woman means.

And it's not only the internal signs of my femininity that I am suddenly analysing with newfound vigour. On a recent holiday I stayed in a hotel with full-length mirrored wardrobes. One morning after my shower, as I sat on the edge of the bed, the towel fell, and I saw my body, in its entirety, for the first time. As a teenager I had stolen my mother's copy of *Our Bodies Ourselves*. I had read it avidly, turning the pages, riveted by its descriptions and diagrams of women's bodies. But when I got to the section that recommended I look at my own body, my own vagina, I shut the book. Why on earth would I want to look at my *vagina*? Having never seen it, I assumed it was ugly. And, amazingly, I had never revised that assumption. Thirty years later, I opened my legs and I looked and I touched and I explored. And it was not ugly.

By some bizarre coincidence, on the flight home, as I skimmed through an airline magazine, a tasteful two-page monochrome spread caught my eye. It was an article on vulval health. I started to read. But quickly I realised that it was not about health at all: it was an ad for labiaplasty. The ad was aimed at women who felt their labia were too big, or too loose, or too unsightly. I turned the page. Later that month, as I flicked through a women's glossy, I spotted another long article on labiaplasty. Though the tone was more sympathetic than that of the airline-magazine ad, I was disheartened. I know that there are women for whom this is a necessary treatment, particularly post-childbirth. But these pieces were not aimed at those scenarios, these were advocating labiaplasty as a cosmetic procedure. I remembered back to my teenage self and my disgust at my own body. I remembered back to when I realised I had cellulite and how, at thirteen, I had added this fact to the list of things to hate about myself. I remembered all the battles over all the years that I had fought in order to accept my body on its own terms. But still I couldn't help it – I read those ads and articles about labiaplasty and I wondered if I had to start hating myself all over again. Was I too big, too loose, too unsightly?

Women are well-rehearsed in the rituals of bodily self-appraisal. We look at the women around us, we look at ourselves, and we compare. Are we alike, are we superior, are we inferior? There is a terrible solidarity to this ritual, given that almost no woman can avoid it. It is like living with a negative cheerleader, this constant background hum that our bodies are not desirable, not acceptable, not normal.

These acts of negative self-comparison most frequently kick in when I look at the hair on my body. From my top lip to my armpits to my legs to my bikini line – I am hairy. And so for even longer than I have been bleeding, I have been shaving. And for almost as long, I have been regretting shaving. But it is not easy to stop. As a sixteen-year-old I rejected the razor, until a friend (clearly a frenemy, but we didn't have the word back then) told me I was being 'gross'. She said she did not want to be seen sitting next to me with 'those legs'. I went back to shaving. Then, in my twenties, I gave it up again. It all went well until one hot day on a crowded subway train my hairy legs were spotted by several children. They pointed at me and *cried*. 'Mummy,' they asked, horrified, 'is that a man?' I smiled at their mother, but she would not meet my eye. I wish I could say I struck a blow for hirsute women everywhere, but I went back to shaving. And, actually, it came as a relief to end the experiment, to have bald legs once more like all the other women. I am torn, you see, between championing the cause of accepting women's body hair and just wanting to fit in.

Sometimes there is no choice, though. I used to shave off the hair that grows in my armpits. But shaving aggravated my eczema, so much so that my skin would get red and raw and infected, and when it was really bad I had to have pus drained from my swollen and throbbing underarm. I have scars from those procedures. I say 'scars' because, each time, though the doctors warned me, I returned to shaving and the cycle of infection began again. I only ended that particular form of self-harm after I fainted while having a painful abcess lanced.

Once I stopped shaving, I was initially ashamed of the hair that grew under my arms. I avoided sleeveless tops. When I had to wear a swimsuit, I kept my arms clamped to my sides. One of my friends told me, consolingly, that she thought the hair was sexy. It was a nice thing to say, but I knew she shaved hers, so it can't have been *that* sexy. Nowadays I barely think of my hairy armpits at all. Until, that is, I see another woman, a woman with visibly smooth underarms, and I realise that my body hair marks me out as different.

My difference came home to me recently when I found myself sitting and watching twenty naked women dancing. The dance was part of a theatre show aimed at challenging porn culture. The point of the naked dancing was to show women expressing themselves physically but not as sexual objects. It was all very good-spirited, and the women seemed to be having fun. So much so that when they asked for audience members to join them, I actually felt tempted. But then I looked again. And – here's the thing – I realised that there was not a single full bush on display. I crossed my legs. Some of the women were neatly shaped, others had more elaborate designs, a few had barely any pubic hair at all. I was puzzled. After all, the women were dancing to defy the patriarchal gaze. So why were they waxed? And why were so many of them so *very* bare, in a show that supposedly confronted the beauty standards of porn? Of course, I hear you say, they were doing it for themselves. No doubt.

It does not matter that I think hair removal is a sadistic, time-consuming and expensive tax on women. It only matters that not fully paying this tax makes me weird. And so I scour magazines and social media in a quest to feel normal. Occasionally I find a public image of a woman with body hair and I feel the pure happiness that comes with external validation. It's not just me! This other woman has hair too! We are a sisterhood of hair! But since it is still so rare for a woman to publicly display anything hairy at all, this sense of joy is equally infrequent.

When I look at women – whether they're dancing naked onstage, or they're in a magazine wearing a bikini – I do not really care if they are smooth or hairy. I do not care about their bodies and what they do with them. I do not care if they think hair is unsightly or unsexy. Because I am not really judging them, I am judging myself. I judge myself for not sufficiently grooming my pubic hair. I judge myself for not shaving my legs as often as I could. I judge myself for not shaving my underarms at all. I judge myself all the time. And this constant act of judgement is the most pointless thing I have ever done.

Sometimes, when I am in the company of more glamorous women, I wonder if I – a white, Western, middle-class, heterosexual, cis-gender woman – am a 'proper girl' at all. Just like that, 'Am I a *proper* girl?' I look from myself to the women around me and I feel that I do not measure up. And then that's when I know that I *am* a girl, that I am *proper*. Because, of course, this paranoia, that I am not feminine enough, not desirable enough, not good enough, is the ultimate performance of femininity. This paranoia is a crucial part of how women are policed. And of how we police ourselves.

A FEW YEARS AGO, while travelling in South East Asia, I treated myself to a full body massage at a beauty salon. It's kind of a funny story, and it may seem incongruous to tell it here, but bear with me. I didn't speak the language and the salon staff didn't speak English, but we smiled and nodded, and a young woman, my masseuse, led me to a private room. She gestured for me to get undressed. I shyly left my underwear on and, seeing this, she laughed. I took my pants off, tried not to think about how hairy I was, and lay on the table. And she started to stroke me, rubbing my sore muscles, and covering my skin with an aromatic paste. When she wrapped me in towels and left me to relax, I exhaled. Okay, I thought, this isn't so bad.

Then I began to warm up. Heat up, really. The paste was spicy and itchy and hot. Within a few minutes, my skin was on fire. The towels were tucked too tightly and I quickly realised that I couldn't move without the risk of throwing myself off the table onto the floor, and the floor looked kind of far away. Think of something else, I told myself. Something not itchy. But I couldn't not think of the itch. 'Breathe,' I told myself, but the deep breathing made the fire burn hotter. I considered calling out for help, for the masseuse to come back and rescue me from being a spicy, itchy, giant kebab. But I imagined the staff's wonder at my inability to enjoy – or endure – the treatment. How exposed would I feel then?

At last the masseuse returned to remove the towels. She helped me off the massage table and led me over to the corner of the room. Where she proceeded to hose me down. With cold water. I shuddered but said nothing, just smiled through teeth that were now chattering. And after I was dry and clothed and walking away, I actually felt great.

But I also felt something else, something unpleasant: I felt humiliated. Not by the staff, or the nakedness, or the paste, or even the hosing down. I was ashamed of my inability to call the masseuse back, to ask for help, to object to the cold water. Too scared of being perceived as weak, I had given up my power and my voice.

And though the spicy massage was a unique event in my life, in some ways it was not an isolated occurrence. Because lined up right next to it are all the other examples of how I have acted as if my body is just too embarrassing. From the fear I have felt at revealing my period to a friend or a boyfriend, to the times I shaved under my arms for the sake of appearance, from the ridiculous to the health-threatening, I have repeatedly denied my body, its importance, and its pain. I have had sex without a condom because I simply could not say the word 'condom' out loud. I have stayed silent during a smear test, trying to ignore the pain caused by a badly wielded speculum. I have stayed equally silent, refusing to allow myself to cry out, during an excruciating ultrasound of my womb, as if I thought my silence might improve the test results.

And I have risked a cancer diagnosis because I could not take my top off. No, that's not true. I could take my top off, but I could not treat what was under it as important. In the shower one morning I felt a lump. I looked up 'breast exam' on the internet and I compared my breast to the one on the screen and I read the description of what a lump felt like and I knew that something was wrong with me. And then, for more than six months, I did nothing. I was afraid it was cancer. But instead of being motivated by that fear, instead of going to the doctor, I stayed quiet. I did not tell my family, my friends, or my boyfriend of the time. And when I finally went for a biopsy, I did so alone. I got lucky. It was benign.

Why do I let embarassment silence me? And why is it so hard for me to treat my body well? Perhaps it is because I associate having a female body with suffering. From the first day that I bled, and I felt crap, and I said nothing, I have gritted my teeth and borne it because I believe that's what other women do, that's what women are expected to do. Because, as a woman, my body is *supposed* to be a site of pain. And pain is something women are meant to be silent about, from the pain of bleeding to the pain of waxing to the pain of not measuring up. Our pain is not important. Our bodies are not important. Pain is the real tax we pay, and poor health is the dividend we reap.

AS I THINK ABOUT THE CONFLUENCE of bodies and silence, I remember back to when pain was something to talk about, when our bodies were the subject of a show-and-tell. Aged seven, I would roll up my trouser leg and narrate the scars – from the dog bite, or from jumping off the shed roof, or from the rusty nail scratch that got infected. Those childhood scars were not just signs of pain, but badges of honour, external proof of internal daring. But as adults our biographies have become rational stories in which we focus on what's in our heads and ignore what's inscribed on our bodies. We might roll up metaphorical sleeves and talk about our heartbreak, our sadness, or our stress. But our bodies are silent, and I think this is perhaps as true for men as it is for women.

It is time to recapture the childhood acceptance of our bodies as a sign of who we are, of what we have done. My body is healthy, it has survived some challenges. It is a body that makes me feel good more than it makes me feel bad. My body enables me to do things. My cellulite thighs are strong, they have carried me up mountains, and I love them. And when I see my lumpectomy scar, a pale white line across my right breast, it makes me happy. The scar is not a sign of weakness, it is a symbol of how I reclaimed my body. I need this scar because I need the reminder that I am the owner of this body.

Sometimes it is hard to look in the mirror. Sometimes it takes years – in my case, decades – to look at ourselves fully. Sometimes the most courageous thing is to look at ourselves without mirrors at all. This kind of nakedness takes work. Getting naked, after all, is not just about how we look on the outside, but admitting how we feel on the inside about how we look on the outside. It is about reversing the dialogue, about throwing out the pretence that I am small and flat and quiet. It is about recognising that my body is not a source of grief, but that all too often the story I have told about it is.

What if my body could tell the story?
What would it say?

I think it would talk about blood. Its mesmerising flow and its ebb. About ending and renewing. I think it would talk about the touch of my fingers and my hands and another's lips. The feel of skin on skin. Wet and slow. Soft and hard. The shock of cold, the pleasure of warmth. I think it would talk about the delight of orgasm and the delight of laughter and the delight of sating hunger. About tasting sharp and spicy, soothing and creamy. I think it would talk about looking out and pulling in. I think it would talk about perfume and stink. About clean and dirty. I think it would talk about illness and recovery, about fortitude and growth. I think it would talk about loss and grief. About standing solo

and holding together. About longevity and transform-
ation. About satisfaction. About happiness. About joy.

I think it would sound strong. I think it would sound
loud. I think it would sound proud.

And I am listening.

And this, this is what it looks like when a woman
bleeds onto the page.

SOMETHING
ABOUT ME

I'M NOT HERE. This is what I'm thinking as his hands are on me, his hands and his mouth and the rest of him, all telling me that he wants to be inside me. *I'm not here.* Because I shouldn't be here. I shouldn't be here at all. I'm only sixteen, my mum doesn't know where I am, it's a school night, I should be tucked up in my own bed, not being fucked on someone else's. *So I'm not here.*

Except, of course, that I am here, or rather I was there, where I shouldn't have been. Ask me now, now that I'm over forty and I'm safe and I have a job and a home and a partner, and I'll tell you that I had a crazy few years as a teenager. Ask me and I'll laugh and say I was maybe a bit out of control. When other people reminisce about being on sports teams or misbehaving on school trips, I might mention the fact that I passed through five secondary schools in the space of three years. It sounds exotic, and people who have only known me in the good years will look slightly surprised, then laugh at the idea that I used to be a wild child. My boyfriend, who knows some of the funnier anecdotes, suggests I write an essay about my younger zany self. But he only knows the quirky version and it's not the whole story. So for a long time, I circle the idea. Why, after all, would I ever tell the story, when to tell it would be to risk the life that I have made in the years since?

I worry away at this question for hours, sitting chin in hand, blank notebook page before me, in the attempt to decide if this is a disaster or a story worth telling. And even if it's worth telling, how could I shape it into something meaningful? I try to start at what I feel is the beginning – *I'm not here* – but that's too late, it wouldn't make sense. Why don't I start at fourteen, when I moved to London? But that's too late too. Maybe I should start with Ireland and my first drink, and my first cigarette, at thirteen? And if I start there, where do I finish? Perhaps at nineteen, with my last cigarette?

And then I realise that this story doesn't start, or end, where I thought it did. There's no one moment of origin

I can easily point to. The chronology is too fraught, and doesn't form year by year, following simple landmarks.

So this may not make sense all the time. But it's what I've got.

AFTER MY PARENTS SEPARATED, we had very little money, a fact I was constantly, achingly aware of. I hated the sense that we were only ever scraping by, I hated that there were no treats, that our car was so old the locks froze shut in winter, that we had no TV, and then later only a tiny black and white one. I hated that I never had more than one pair of shoes, and that those shoes were never the branded ones the other kids in my class had. I hated that I wore cast-offs from older or bigger children. Most of all, I hated that we ate the same cheap food repeatedly, an endless litany of grey-brown mince and watery potatoes that, each mealtime, filled me with revulsion. And then, at ten years old, I discovered the power of not eating.

Most weekdays my mum sent me to school with my lunch, usually a sandwich and an apple. But some mornings, short on time, or bread, or something to put between the slices, she told me I could eat one of the sandwiches that came in the bag. Every child received a free daily carton of milk. The carton came in a slab and slung on top, like some sort of afterthought, was a clear plastic bag of sandwiches. They were mostly ham, and some were cheese, the ham slimy and the cheese plasticky, both heavily smeared with butter. I hated butter in sandwiches (I still do). Though I think now that they were probably put in the bags in neat stacks, by the time they got to my classroom they were always a mismatched pile. To get a sandwich involved reaching into the greasy bag and picking out each component. They managed to feel both stale and soggy and, in winter, warm from the radiator.

The boys drank the milk, and some, after playing football all lunch break, would eat the sandwiches too. But girls didn't eat them, or not as far as I could see, and certainly not the girls that mattered. It was bad enough that I was already the kid in hand-me-downs, including those from a not-very-nice taller girl in my class (our mums were friends). 'Oh,' she would say, 'I used to have a jumper just like that.' 'Oh,' she would say, 'I think that *was* my jumper.' Under her gaze, I could never have picked up a free sandwich, no matter how hungry I was. So on those days that my mum didn't have time to make me a lunch, I simply didn't eat. And then – is this where the story starts? – I stopped eating those sandwiches she did make. I squashed them down to the bottom of my bag, where they mouldered and smelled. I satisfied myself by eating the daily apple. Then I stopped eating the apple too. I found I had a talent for hunger.

Once, being driven home after school, I told the car-pool mum that I hadn't eaten anything at all that day. And – this was the punchline – I wasn't even hungry. She told me not to be stupid. I elatedly insisted that no, really, I didn't eat anything, all day. And then, believing me, she made me eat the leftover crusts from her daughter's lunch. This was not the reaction I wanted. She was not filled with admiration at my achievement of will over appetite. I choked back my tears, chewing resentfully, and decided that I would not expose myself again. I would not tell anyone about my victory over weakness. I would just do it. And this actually made not eating even better. Because now I had something, a secret weapon, that was mine only. Not eating, I felt clean and light. And powerful.

I had no friends in school, but then that's probably already apparent from the kind of story I'm telling here. I misunderstood how to make friends: I talked too loudly, or I cared too much what they thought about me. I didn't know the right rules.

I had always been a thin child, and no one really noticed that I started to get a bit thinner. I ate a few mouthfuls of breakfast cereal on days when my mum demanded it. If she forced me to eat more, I would make myself throw up. One day, when I had to finish a whole bowl of cereal, I threw up on the hall carpet, just to make a point. It was too much hassle for my mum, one thing too many, on a morning when she was already running late. 'God, isn't it enough?' she said. 'Get in the car.' I wasn't quite sure what she meant by 'isn't it enough?' and I feared I'd gone too far. But after that the pressure to eat breakfast lessened.

I always ate one full meal each day at dinner time and so I never got dangerously ill or thin. I did get sick all the time and I fell quite a lot, a combination of clumsiness and faintness. In fact, I was in and out of the emergency department in the Children's Hospital, often with sprained wrists or ankles, getting to know the faces and names of the nurses and admission clerks. I remember one injury that was so bad that my mum had to take a week off work to look after me. We spent the days making a cardboard doll's house together, and she cooked me my favourite foods. It was a rare period of calm and closeness. I ate. I began to feel better. When I went back to school at the end of the week I was briefly popular for allowing the other kids to race with my crutches. But soon enough I went back to not eating. I stayed at my desk during lunch break, with a book.

I was increasingly anxious. I started not sleeping. I would lie in bed, dissecting and rephrasing everything I had said during the day, reflecting on everything I had got wrong. At this stage I was probably eleven. My mum took me to the doctor, concerned at the dark circles under my eyes and my constant tiredness. In the consultation room, the GP asked my mum to leave us alone, and then he asked me if there was anything I was particularly worried about. I said no. I don't remember the other questions, but I do remember feeling that if I said nothing, they wouldn't find me out. When my mum came back in, the doctor commented on my thinness, and asked if I had an appetite. He weighed me on one of those old-fashioned scales with weights and balances. I watched his thick fingers move the slider. 'She's underweight,' he said, to the room. And I thought to myself, 'This is it, this is the moment I get noticed.' My mum then recounted how greedily I ate when I was given my favourite foods, like a chicken sandwich slathered with mayo. They laughed.

In the car, Mum asked me if I had told the doctor what I was worrying about. I stared at my lap, and shook my head. She got annoyed and told me that she had had to take the afternoon off work, and that doctors were expensive. Her voice was sharp with money worries. I resolved that in future I would not tell her if I hadn't slept. And that I would not tell her that I just wouldn't let myself sleep. That it was another rule, another form of control, another punishment.

I SPENT YEARS following my hunger regime. But when I got to secondary school, I needed more to get through the day. One morning, at the school assembly, I started to feel weak. First my sight went, but I could still hear the announcements and I could stand in my place, swaying forward a little. Then a loud buzzing filled my ears and there was total blackness. I let go. The girl who stood next to me in the line told me afterwards that I made a loud bang as I hit the parquet. The school matron was dismissive when I confessed that I'd 'forgotten' to have breakfast. In fact, my constant refusal of breakfast had become such a battleground at home, that my mum had recently pursued me to the bus stop, still in her dressing-gown, waving a piece of toast.

For the rest of the assembly the whole school was made to sit on the dusty floor. Afterwards, older girls feigned concern, putting an arm around me, claiming me as a mascot, and for the remainder of the year I attained some slight celebrity, being pointed out as the girl who fainted. At least, at this point, I had friends. By thirteen I had begun to find people who seemed to like me – who did, in fact, like me. But it took me a long time to let myself believe that. Perhaps the most corrosive aspect of a lonely life is not the time spent alone, but the time spent in a crowd, feeling left out.

My new friends noticed my thinness. Everyone did. Other parents and teachers commented on it. When it was seen as a problem, I was called 'skinny', a label that thrilled me. Mostly I was described in coded ways that I knew proclaimed thinness a 'good thing', with words like 'slim' or 'slender'. I was smart at school, could act confidently (for which, read 'loud'), and tell funny stories. But being thin, with jutting elbows and a fretboard of ribs, was the only skill I valued.

I knew, at this stage, the effect of my body on others. And I found new ways to exploit my body to generate further kinds of emotional pay-off. I developed a social life and started to go to other kids' houses after school and then weekend parties. I longed to be cool. I would stand on the edge of groups of kids who were talking and laughing and making out and yearn to be included. As I continued to hang around, I started smoking, copied the walks of the other girls, sashayed my hips in what I hoped was a seductive manner. Around boys I liked, I smiled coyly, even stared openly. It was one way of being seen myself. At one party, I followed a boy outside when he beckoned to me, then I cringed in shame as he laughed at me, shouting to all his friends that I was desperate. But desperation, in itself, can be attractive. I learned that if boys wanted to use my body I could rediscover that early feeling of triumph and lightness that I'd previously only felt through not eating. That I found the encounters themselves fairly distasteful was neither here nor there.

I remember my hymen breaking, the blood in my underwear, after an over-eager boy put most of his hand up me. It hurt but I only silently grimaced, afraid of being heard and laughed at by the other girls. I assumed he'd done it before. I assumed it was what the cool girls did. In fact, it probably was what the cool girls did because none of us, not a one, was confident enough to say no to what seemed expected. To object would be to declare ourselves, to him and all his friends, frigid. Which was even worse than being 'easy'. I know now that all I really wanted was affection – to be touched or held with love, with understanding, with kindness. And yet this was an impossible ask. I was so filled with the need and wanting of it, and so transparently so, that I think it must have been hard, sometimes, for people to look at me without flinching.

***

Something About Me

WHEN I WAS FOURTEEN my mum's job took me and my sister to London. My father, an infrequent contributor to our lives anyway, stayed in Dublin. London meant a new school and a whole new level of opportunity. It also meant a whole new group of friends, girls at my school, who seemed daring and brave and cool. And who mistook me for cool too. They let me hang out with them, and together we started going to clubs. I told my mum I was staying at another girl's house and in this new city, where she knew no one's parents, she did not realise I was lying. And soon this new kind of lying became second nature, the only way to get what I wanted.

One Friday night at a club I was flirting with a late-twenty-something man and he asked my age. I told him nineteen. I told him I was an art student. This was what I always said, because it sounded impressive, though I would have been totally stuck had anyone ever asked me what kind of art I studied. After kissing me, he drew back, checked my face and asked my age again. I smiled and said seventeen. He blanched, backed away and fled. When I returned to the dance floor and told my friends we roared with laughter. The sap. We were bulletproof. We were fifteen.

I killed the girl in hand-me-downs. I became the audacious girl, in a uniform of lipstick and short skirts, the girl in the club, the girl who knew where the party was. I was so high and having so much fun that I never missed the book-girl I used to be. I had free gig tickets, backstage passes, my name on the guestlist to a different club every night of the week. It seems insane now but two of my best friends and I gave out 'business' cards with our names, phone numbers, and the slogan 'Made in Heaven, Raised in Hell'. Free drinks at the bar. A spot in the DJ box. VIP areas. All it took was to be under-age, in a tiny dress, and to play willing to please. And oh, did I do that act well. Because I was willing to please. I wore my mum's old dresses, which she'd saved from the 1970s. I cut them down so that they barely covered my ass. I donned, in what I thought was a spec-tacular move, a nun's habit, with the bottom sheared off and a zip that ran all the way down the front. When my mum challenged my outfits, I grudgingly covered up, but this only added to the game. Leaving the house I wore a long top and long skirt. But as soon as I got to the club, I disrobed in the foyer, often for an audience, handing my outer layers to one of the bouncers, reveal-ing the tiny outfit below.

My new lifestyle did not end at nightclubs. I went to music festivals and revelled in their lack of rules. I went to one festival where it rained and rained and every-thing was drowned in mud. On the last day, when a

dishevelled guy said he could take me backstage to meet
Nirvana, I abandoned my borrowed tent, and my bor-
rowed sleeping bag, and my clothes and everything I'd
brought. I didn't even say goodbye to the friends I'd
arrived with. I didn't care. I stood next to Kurt Cobain
at the bar. He was drinking what looked like a gin and
tonic and smoking light cigarettes. I dismissed him as a
lightweight and turned away. After all, I drank neat
vodka and smoked high-tar only. I followed the dishev-
elled guy on to a posh hotel, where we partied with a
group of music promoters, broke furniture and ran up a
sky-high bar bill. We slowed down only long enough to
shave off the eyebrows of those who'd passed out. And
then we got kicked out.

I chose this moment to ring my mum from the
courtesy telephone. It was not yet 6am. She answered
blearily. When I drunkenly slurred the name of the
hotel, she said that she'd actually been there herself a
few weeks earlier, at a work conference. Wasn't that
funny, she said. I agreed and hung up. Even now I have
no idea what I wanted from that call.

I caught up with the others and walked with them
towards the train station. Along the way we somehow
managed to shoplift, of all things, a pair of waterproof
river waders. We laughed and laughed. I ended up at
one of the stranger's houses, and stayed there for a few

days. I didn't go home for a week in total. I had left the festival with an entirely different group of people than I arrived with. The person who owned the tent that I'd abandoned, my sister who owned the sleeping bag, and my friends, who I'd left without warning, none of them were speaking to me. I had a hangover that registered only a few levels above death. I thought my life was great.

By this point I was, literally, a poster wild child. I appeared on a national television talk show as a prime example, displayed to scare middle-class parents. I chose to wear a t-shirt, on which I wrote the name of a recent ex-boyfriend, followed by the words 'is a tosser'. My dad still recounts this anecdote, proudly. But on that show, I sat next to another featured guest, a mum whose son had died from huffing aerosols. She was quiet, nice, heartbroken. She'd had no idea her son was so at risk, and she was on the show to warn other parents. Even through the ten-foot-deep insulation of the self-absorbed teenager, I felt compassion for her. And then I briefly wondered if my own mum wasn't quite as blasé as I thought she was. I remembered one evening, soon after our move to London, when she had paused at the open door to my bedroom, and asked what I was doing. I was sitting on the floor, with my back to the radiator, just staring into space. I started to cry. 'I'm lonely,'

I said. 'I know,' she said, then she shrugged and continued up the stairs to bed. I assumed she did not care. And yet if she had crossed that threshold, had comforted me, what would I have done? I would have shouted at her to get out. Had she tried to hug me, I would have stiffened my body and told her in my coldest voice to get away and stop touching me.

Sitting in the television studio, though I connected the bereaved mum to my own mum, I did not connect her son's fate to mine. After all, I didn't inhale aerosol fumes to get high. I took drugs, but I had rules. I never touched crack or heroin. I thought that this boundary, marking out the limits of my wildness, would keep me safe. I really thought I was bulletproof.

But there were danger signs even I couldn't avoid seeing. I went for a weekend to Manchester with a DJ I'd been flirting with for months. He'd given me lifts in his car, given me presents, given me drink, given me drugs. He was over twice my age. He loved to parade me at parties, to announce to all and sundry that I was jailbait, or sometimes to pretend that he was my father, before kissing me, or licking my face. But I had never been alone with him. In Manchester, after his guest-slot at a student bar, we went to the hotel. And I realised I had made a horrible mistake. He was aggressive. He wanted it rough and when I said that I didn't like it like that, he said that he had paid for everything, and so I owed him. Somehow I placated him, feeding him drinks from the mini-bar. When he passed out, I locked myself in the bathroom. I sneaked out in the morning when I heard the hotel maids in the corridor. I walked to the station, dodged the ticket inspectors on the train, and got back to London. The next time I saw that man was at the usual Friday club, when he started throwing empty pint glasses in my direction, shouting warnings to other men that I was a tease. The bouncers stood and watched as the glass shattered around me.

I got a head injury some months later when I was hit in the face with a beer bottle on the dance floor of a nightclub. The woman who hit me claimed I was dancing too close to her boyfriend. Head wounds are bleeders and the bathroom floor became a lake of red as the blood hit the wet tiles. The club promoter was concerned, but also needed me off the premises. 'What age are you, really, Emilie?' Even bleeding, I was not unaware of the irony behind the question, given that I was on a guestlist for his club, that he'd bought me countless drinks, and that he'd tried to sleep with me many times. He knew I was underage. Rather than answer, I left. A concerned group brought me to A&E. I returned home, in the early hours of Christmas Eve, with stitches that stretched into my hairline.

And I still hardly ate. In fact, not eating was a positive advantage for my lifestyle. I had no money of my own, so eating out was hardly an option. I spent time with men who would tell me how great my (undernourished) body was but who never offered to buy me dinner. After I got sick of nightclubs, I started hanging out a lot with friends in squats and at raves, existing on a diet of Mars bars and wraps of speed. My lunch money, which my mum always set aside, usually went on sugar-rich alcohol, enabling me to skip yet more meals. After years of not eating, I was constitutionally prepared for this rhythm. But it was still exhausting.

And it was cold. We spent a great deal of time, me and my friends, being cold. Actually cold, as in shivering, because the temperature was low and we were outside and not wearing sufficient clothes. We shivered outside clubs, at bus stops, smoking cigarettes, queueing for gigs, waiting for the Tube, waiting for friends, waiting for men. We stamped our feet, hands pushed tightly down into our pockets, arms clamped to our sides. For a while, before we knew people on the scene, we had found a halfway house in a bank foyer off Oxford Street, where the card swipe was broken and the door opened to a gentle shove. We'd sit there for hours, till we were sore and cramped, and it was light enough to go home. It was warmer than staying on the street, though not much. I briefly had a boyfriend who lived in a room over a tattoo parlour, and he'd let us stay there some nights. Even if we wanted to go home, it was not simple. Emerging from north London clubs, we caught night-buses, cutting south through the city to Trafalgar Square, but there was always another wait in the cold for the one that would take you home, and the bus stop was a lonely place. One night, as the bus approached the Trafalgar terminus, the kindly-seeming driver asked me and my friend if we wanted to stay on the bus, to wait in its warmth. He pulled into a side street. Then he turned the bus engine off, the lights too, and when he moved towards us he suddenly seemed less kindly. He'd seen our child travel cards, so there was no point in warning him we were underage. Our youth was part of the kick. As he got closer, we screamed and banged on the windows. He cursed us and pulled the door lever.

Another night I found money on the street. I hailed a cab. But he pulled into a side street too. Central door locking. I told him that I had a mum and a little sister at home, waiting for me. But he only told me that I was a bad girl. He showed me his aluminium baseball bat. He watched me in the rear-view mirror. I could tell he didn't think anyone was waiting – because what other kind of girl is standing by herself on a kerb in north London at 4am? He was only into looking though. He stroked the bat, then left it on the floor of the passenger footwell. He started the engine and drove back to the main road, kicking me out so that I had to walk the rest of the way. When I got home, the hall light was on. Mum always left it on for me. I see that light now as a sign that she was waiting, worrying, all of those nights. That she only half slept, alert until the sound of my key in the door. I wish I could erase many of the consequences of my actions but, more than anything, I wish I could erase that worry.

FOR A WHILE, I was able to act out my badness without anyone noticing at school. I kept my uniform in a locker. I could get an early Tube looking like a shard of last night, yet by assembly I seemed like any other schoolgirl in her regulation blouse and skirt. But in my second year in London my system to escape detection began to break down. Increasingly the hangovers made it impossible to get in before the first bell, and once I'd missed that, the rest of the day seemed hardly worth it. I started to skip weeks at a time. And when I did turn up, there was trouble. One day I was spotted by the P.E. teacher and she began a tirade about my missing all my games classes. I was on the brink of being taken to the headmistress's office when my science teacher rescued me. Though I had also missed several weeks of her classes, she insisted to the games teacher that I was in fact a new pupil, and that since I had only just joined the school I couldn't have missed anything. She ushered me into her classroom, showed me where to sit and gave me a fresh new exercise book. At the time, I was convinced that this teacher was losing her marbles, that she genuinely didn't recognise me or realise that I was a continuing pupil. Now, though, I tend to think that she was well aware of who I was, and chose to shield me with a barefaced lie from a notoriously angry and unstable teacher; she kept up the 'new girl' pretence in order to protect both of us. I was grateful. Yet I never went to another of her classes. In fact, I never had another science class ever again. It was easier, in the end, to just drop out.

I was not alone, my two best friends had the same trajectory. More and more days missed. More assignments not completed. Calling into school as if it were a social club, then out again. There were a few teachers who tried to reach us, but in the main both teachers and administrators washed their hands of us. And who could blame them, when we did all we could to get expelled? Yet looking back now, though I see what a nightmare our behaviour was, I am stunned to realise just how young, and just how vulnerable, we were. One of my friends had severe dyslexia. Though she was in many ways the smartest, and certainly the most resourceful of us, she consistently failed tests and was pushed down the school streaming system. Was it any wonder that she chose not to turn up for her exams? Another friend left school at the same time as me. Her father was abusive to her. This fact was as clear as day to anyone with any sense. But no one did anything. We might have seemed all-knowing, but we were really so innocent. What we needed was help. What we needed was protection. Not to be just let go.

Without school as a destination, it was difficult to find places to stay out all day. Because unless you're rich, the wild-child lifestyle is not just cold but also boring. At a loss for what to do, I started to feign illness so that I could stay home with daytime television for company. It was blissful by contrast. But pretty soon my mum insisted I stop malingering and go back to classes. I couldn't. I repeated it over and over, a chant, 'I can't, I can't, I can't.' I was, in fact, right. The next day she went in to meet the headmistress. It turned out I had attended too few days to be allowed to sit my intermediate exams at a state school or, indeed, to be admitted to another comprehensive school at all, unless I repeated the year. The deputy headmistress suggested that we should all cut our losses and that I could get a job. She smiled – perhaps McDonald's? Mum wouldn't accept defeat so easily, so the only option left was for her to find the money to send me to a private school.

I tried out, Goldilocks-style, for three new schools. At the first, though I turned on my best and nicest smile for the interview, and made sure to mention my interest in joining the choir, the headmistress saw right through me. She did not return my mum's calls. The second gave me a day's trial, but the day did not go well. There was some suggestion that I had made the Italian teacher cry. I was used to being in large, noisy classrooms where a certain amount of anarchy was normal. I was used to having to shout to be heard, or being left to my own devices at the back of the room. I was used to a school where no disciplinary action was taken when my class conspired to lock the art teacher in the supply room. This new, posh, quiet-girl school, with its policies on which side of the corridor to walk, was beyond me, and I wasn't invited back.

At the third school, they asked me to do a simple mathematics question on probability, which I answered correctly. As the headmaster filled out various forms, I interrupted him to ask that my first name not be spelled with a 'y' at the end. At previous schools, staff had taken an almost gleeful satisfaction in scratching out the way I spell my name, and in making me write it out 'correctly' as punishment for 'defacing' my exercise books. The headmaster looked at me a moment. 'You can spell your name any way you want.' He explained that there were only two rules – first, turn up and, second, do the work. There was a zero tolerance policy for breaking them, which initially had both me and my mum worried. But they also scheduled classes to begin after ten, permitted cigarette breaks and allowed you to bring coffee to class. All teachers and pupils were addressed by their first names. There were only six students per class. And, crucially, the school had no uniform or dress code. No more locker-room costume changes for me.

I was relieved and, oh my God, was my mum relieved. Even so, the change of school was not all plain sailing. The other kids were all rich and so I was back to feeling poor. Many of them were rich bullies. Most of them had, like me, failed at surviving in the mainstream system. One morning, a boy turned to me in the hallway and told me to get back into the gutter. A few years later I might have tried out the Wildean line about lying in the gutter but looking at the stars. Instead, I told him to fuck off. I continued to stay out all night, drinking and taking drugs, but I managed, despite this, to follow the rules; I turned up and I handed in my coursework.

I did a creative writing class and received praise for the first time in a long time. I took my intermediate exams. I registered for my final exams. At the encouragement of a favourite teacher, I started thinking about the prospect of third level. It turns out that the ambition of the nerd-girl dies hard. It wasn't an overnight transformation, and it wasn't always even a conscious choice, but I gradually began to pay attention to my life. And, because of this, I made it through. You know that fact, of course, because you're reading this now.

I could end the story there. I could say that education saved me, and in many ways that would be true. But it would only be part of the truth. Because there are things I've left out. And if I'm to tell it, then this is the part where the story turns, and where I find myself, again, asking why I'm telling it at all. Let me pause, and just look out the window for a while. Let me stand up and walk away from the desk. Let me take a minute.

AT FIFTEEN, with two of my friends, I ran away from home.

We left notes saying we would not be back. We took sleeping bags and all our savings, about £12. We hoped, if we hung around in the city centre, that we'd meet someone who would let us stay at their place. We did, inevitably, attract attention, from a skinhead who offered to put us up somewhere if we went with him 'right now'. But for all our bravado, we preferred sleeping in shop doorways to the risk of getting in a van with a man who could drive us who knew where.

Falling asleep on the street is scary. Waking up is shameful. The people who worked in the shops and offices we slept outside stepped over us in the mornings. During the day, we begged for money. This was initially also shaming, but could be a surprising illustration of people's generosity too. One smiling man bought us all ice-cream sundaes, delivered with the line, 'Don't say I never give you anything.' We were euphoric. But that kind of human contact was rare, and as we got tired and our voices grew whiny, we seemed increasingly invisible to all those passers-by.

One night we took refuge in a hostel for homeless children. At the hostel we got a hot meal, and forms to fill out, and guidance on how to get on housing lists. During our interviews, discreet queries were made about domestic violence, about family abuse, about gang membership. We were offered counselling. The staff were sympathetic, though the other kids knew we were bullshitting when we said we were sixteen and, it felt to me, they guessed we were also bullshitting about our reasons for being on the street. In planning to run away, my friends and I had talked about how unhappy we felt at home, how much freer we would be elsewhere. We had said that running away was a radical thing that other girls would talk about but not have the guts to carry out. We had thought it would give us some kind of power. It was apparent within a few days of sleeping rough, begging and trying to keep warm in train station waiting rooms, that we were woefully mistaken. I wanted to go home. I was embarrassed, as my two friends still refused to go back. But this was one of those rare moments when I acted in my own best interests, and not in order to win a popularity vote. Because I had known, even as I had packed my bag to leave my mum's house, that I couldn't run away from what was really wrong. I was not battered at home. I was not treated cruelly. I had no real reason for running away. I was just lonely. I was just unhappy. I was just lost.

My younger sister was as affected as I was by being in this family, though she dealt with it by being the sweetest, most emotionally open child you could ever meet. It seemed that she wanted to be the opposite of me in temperament, like so many other younger children seeking to distance themselves from their older sibling. Yet she wasn't distant, she was always hugging me and reassuring me. After I ran away, she was suddenly the only child in the house. A fact I did not even momentarily pause to consider on my way out the door. But I realised it with full force when I came home. I rang the doorbell and my sister came running and wrapped herself around me in the tightest grip I've ever felt. She was crying. She looked up at me with big sad eyes, and asked, 'Why did you leave us?' And I had no answer. I hadn't anticipated that she'd miss me, or that she'd be pleased that I'd come home, or that she needed me to be there and not leave. In the selfishness I felt was sanctioned by my own emotional pain, I hadn't considered anyone else's needs.

Recalling the hurt and confusion in my sister's voice at that moment, I realise that we both needed the same thing: some promise of unconditional love, some security, unavailable to either of us. And I think that maybe, in the end, we got it from each other. Two years later, when I had screwed up again and feared my mum would kick me out, my sister promised she'd keep the screw-up a secret. She told me she'd still love me, no matter what. Then she came to me with her bank book and, with great seriousness, offered to sign over all her savings so that I'd be okay. I couldn't take it, so I hugged her, I reassured her, I smiled and joked until the worry left her eyes.

***

BUT I WAS NOT REALLY OKAY. And so there is another bit of the story that needs telling, of all the other nights I didn't come home.

This is how it goes. I went to nightclubs, sometimes with friends, but sometimes by myself because my friends were tired of going out all the time in search of attention. At clubs I flirted with the stranger at the bar. After so many drinks that I would have to concentrate *really* hard, gripping the edge of the bar itself, just in order to stay standing up, the stranger would ask me what I'd like to do. Slurring my words, I would ask if there was vodka back at his place. He would smile as an answer. He'd say we could take a cab. There were no phones to text anyone, no mobile apps to order my own taxi, no HPV vaccine, because all this was a million years ago. So I would end up in this strange man's flat with a mug of vodka and no way out. The man may have thought that I gave him everything when my nakedness was there, in the room, gooseflesh. And sure, my body was there. But I was miles away. I had one thought only, reverberating through me, saving me but damning me too. I removed myself through this mantra: *I am not here*.

I thought I knew the value of what I traded – my adolescent body – and I thought that I was on the winning end of the bargain. But what it really meant was that I put no value on myself at all. And so the separation of body and self that I engineered, which began years earlier when I stopped eating normally, was made complete by these encounters. And they hurt. Physically. Mentally. Emotionally. They hurt. Every time. All the times.

I maintained a happy-go-lucky façade, but inwardly became cold, sensationless. I distanced myself from anything emotionally problematic. I basically shut down. Instead of talking to the people I was with, I continued the internal dialogue I had begun as a sleepless child, in which I would witness, as if from a great distance, my own actions, accompanied by a relentlessly fault-finding commentary. Though I have managed over the years to get away from most of my self-destructive traits, that particular dialogue is still with me. It is still what keeps me awake at night.

At some point during these years, my mum took me to a family counselling session. The two of us sat with a therapist in her basement room. She asked me if there was anything I wanted to say to my mum, and I shook my head. My response to every question was to say I was fine. I had, of course, so much that I needed to say and perhaps if I'd been in the room by myself, I could have said some of it. But, mostly, I think that I lacked the vocabulary. I could not say 'I'm lonely' or 'I'm unhappy', or, what it all came down to, '*I am worthless.*' To put my fears into words seemed not only emotionally impossible, but outside the range of how I could talk about myself. Not having a language, or a voice, to articulate what it was that made me feel so alone was catastrophic. And because no one else used these words either, or intervened to help me say them for myself, the silence was complete.

At seventeen, I started to have panic attacks. The air would disappear from my lungs. I'd gasp and try to run outside, desperately seeking oxygen, and then I'd faint (always with the fainting). During one attack, at a concert, I was pulled by security from the crowd and into the backstage area. A medic listened to my chest, my frantic heartbeat and ragged breath, and gave me a shot of adrenaline. It stopped the hyperventilating and then it made me retch. I told people, worried people, that these episodes were asthma attacks. One person accused me of attention-seeking, but I really couldn't breathe.

I turned eighteen. And I gave up drugs. The speed I was taking was increasingly messing up my insides. I couldn't sleep or sit still for cramps. I shook. I felt ravaged. I woke up one morning and, before I got out of bed, I took a hit of acid. This isn't right, I thought, even as I did it. So I faced a choice: all or nothing. I chose nothing. At first, friends thought this was brilliant.

They would say about me, almost bragging, that 'Emilie has given up drugs.' But without the drugs – surprise, surprise – the rest wasn't so bearable. The warehouse raves that I'd moved on to, and the squats I stayed in, were desolate places while straight. And the novelty wore off for my friends who didn't want someone so sober hanging around. I made them paranoid.

Besides, my core group of friends had dispersed. Some who had loved indie and grunge clubs just didn't enjoy the raves. Some had realised they had to study if they wanted those famous 'options' beyond school. Others had already dropped out and, too young for proper welfare benefits, were living on what they could beg and, eventually, income from dealing. Some had been moved to stricter foster homes. Some had got pregnant. I started staying home on Saturday nights. I was back to being the not-popular girl. But at this stage I knew that loneliness was not the worst thing.

A close friend tried suicide by overdose, unsuccessfully, several times, though her bulimia nearly did the trick. A girl I met at a club told me that when her parents found her cutting her wrists, her mother put salt in the wounds to dissuade her from trying again. One friend had taken so much acid he had no short-term memory. Another wandered off from a party one night, disappeared for several weeks and, though he reappeared at a squat, was never the same gentle boy he was before. At least he was alive.

Because not all of us made it. This is a screaming, painful, shitty fact.

Not all of us made it.

A girl I knew at school, who was bright and funny and kind and generous, was also unstable and unhappy, and she was sectioned by her parents. At some point during her incarceration, she hanged herself. A boy I'd known since I'd first moved to London was abandoned to foster care when his father left the country and never returned. When this boy turned eighteen, and was released to live in a halfway hostel, he took a fatal overdose. Among my friends, their deaths were cried over, whispered about, experienced as a physical shock. It was said that my schoolfriend's parents had not visited her once in the psychiatric unit. All I could think about was the last time I'd seen her, laughing on a night out, and talking about a band we both loved. I hadn't really seen the boy in years, but I sometimes spoke to him on the phone. He'd call when he felt lonely, though the foster home limited the calls to five minutes. Their deaths were the most and least real things I'd ever known. I've never really processed them. I still expect to see them someday, to catch sight of the backs of their heads in a crowd.

***

Something About Me

THERE ARE OTHER THINGS that I have not processed.

When I first moved to London, and was still going to school like a regular fourteen-year-old, I would get the Tube home every day, during rush hour. One afternoon, standing in a crowded train, I felt a man rub himself up against me. I was shocked, but found a way to say, quite loudly, 'Please stop touching me.' He stopped, briefly. But then, after the next station, he started again and I started crying. I wasn't crying quietly, I was really sobbing. I was a child, in school uniform, and surrounded by adults, but not a single person said or did anything. At the next stop I got off the train, pushing past those silent commuters. I stood on the platform of Gloucester Road for a long time, trying to stop the convulsive tears, to catch my breath. No one said anything.

By the time I was eighteen, I had heard the statistic that one in four women will be raped. I looked around. Were my friends and I included in this figure, or were we all miraculously exempt? I thought of the Tube event and all the other times men had made unwanted advances. I thought of times I had not wanted sex but I had complied. But I had never been raped. It was not until I was thirty-nine and in the audience at a feminist event where women were encouraged to tell their personal stories, that I rethought my certainty about that statement. *I had never been raped*. I sat in that crowded hall, listening to accounts of serious sexual violence, and suddenly two very clear memories surfaced. Overwhelmed, I left the hall and stood crying on the street outside. Because I had been raped.

The attacks did not happen on a dark street, as I had been trained to think of all rape. I knew both the attackers. I talked to them afterwards. I got up and walked away. Apart from a few bruises I was left physically unscathed. And I did not go to the police. So for all these years I thought of these two assaults as just those times I was forced to have sex against my will. The two times that I did say no, and it didn't matter.

The first time, it was my boyfriend. He was two years or so older than me, maybe seventeen. One night after a club, he walked me back to my friend's house. I let myself in with a borrowed key. It was winter and cold so he asked if he could come in too. I told him to go home, that I was only going to bed, but he pushed open the door and stepped into the house. Then I told him to leave, but he just smiled. So I said goodnight and went upstairs hoping that was the end of it. He followed me. He pulled me into an empty bedroom. And then he forced me onto the bed and pulled my tights and pants down and pushed himself into me. I said no. Actually, I said, 'Don't,' but the meaning is the same. He had his hand on my throat, making it hard to breathe or speak, but I didn't want to call out more loudly anyway in case I woke the other people in the house. I thought they would be angry with me for letting him in. As he thrust harder, I gasped and cried and asked him to stop. And then I just gritted my teeth, tears flowing silently, knowing that it would be over soon. When he was finished, he wasted no time, just pulled out and zipped up and walked out of the room. I heard the front door slam. I dragged up my pants and tights and wrapped the duvet around me. I had had sex with this boy before, consensual sex. So this couldn't be rape. I continued to see him for another few weeks before he dumped me for another girl.

The second time was a couple of years later. I went to a friend's flat and had dinner with him and his house-guest, an older man, who was visiting from Ireland. He and I bonded over a bottle of red wine and our shared experiences of anti-Irish racism in London. When my friend went to bed, we stayed up talking. But then he forced himself on me, all six feet-plus of him, holding me down with his forearm across my chest, and his hand pushing my face into the sofa cushions. When he went to sleep I pulled myself out from under his bulk and crawled into my friend's bedroom, lying on the floor till it was light and I could escape.

At the time, I rationalised both of these assaults not as rapes, but as the inevitable outcomes of my actions and my lifestyle. Though I would have been horrified if anyone had ever said to me that a short skirt gave a man a licence to rape a woman, in effect this was what I had internalised. I took my punishment because I had a strong sense of having done something wrong, having knowingly broken the good-girl rules. I denied what had happened to me because it was the only way I knew how to survive.

I still struggle to know what to do with this personal history. I struggle with how to categorise the experiences, and even whether to use the term 'rape'. I am wary of minimising the violence done to other women during rape, and I'm still not sure that I get to claim that experience, not sure if I suffered enough to deserve the label. Added to that, I feel guilt at not reporting these men in case my silence enabled them to do something worse to someone else. But who, really, would I have reported them to? I had no sense, whatsoever, that I would be believed or taken seriously by anyone. I still don't.

After the second rape I asked the man why he'd done it. He turned his head, and this I remember, crystal clear, The Prodigy was playing on the stereo, and he said, 'It's just something about you, a vibe you give off.'

I kept that damaging explanation with me, inside me, for decades. It was something about me. I cried at the feminist meeting all those years later when I realised that the 'vibe' I gave off was simply being young and vulnerable and female.

I WAS DAMAGED, but I made it through. I did my end-of-school exams. I got a place at an Irish university, where I finally felt at home. I went to lectures and seminars and met people who thought, like I did, that reading and talking about books was a good way to spend your time. I kept some old habits, drinking oceans of free beer during the open-bar events, but rapidly ditched the others. And I started to play a new game, or rather a new variation on the old game of fitting in. This game's rules consisted of pretending that I had not, in fact, spent years going clubbing, taking drugs, and going home with random men. My new friends seemed so much more innocent, so I played along.

What college really gave me, though, was a form of control over my life. I was where I wanted to be, doing what I wanted to do, and as this knowledge took hold, the need to control my eating lessened. I started eating two, then three, meals a day. I would like to say that I never regress. But it's easier to write about an eating disorder in the past tense than to actually be past it. Even after years, now, of eating normally, I live in a house without a full-length mirror, or a set of scales. I am unable to face my body. I hate this fact, even as I admit it here. I hate that it undermines my sense of recovery. I hate that it connects me, backwards, to my younger, pained self. I hate that it expresses a persistently negative relationship between my body and desire.

Desire. That word has changed its meaning. To own my body, my skin and nerve-endings, as a site of pleasure – my own, and not just someone else's – and to have *agency* has been a long transformation, and one that still feels radical. Once, in my twenties, I was at a family-planning clinic to get a repeat prescription for the pill. The dispensing nurse smiled and then talked to me about foreplay, and the length of time it takes for women to climax, and she told me that most women can't achieve orgasm through penetration alone. I endured the consultation, blushing every time she talked about sexual pleasure, but this was life-changing information. Sex, it turns out, is meant to be – it is – fun. It does not shake the whole wide world, or revolutionise anyone else's sexual politics, but this different attitude to my physical self, only fully discovered in my thirties really, has shaken my world and, often, my body. *I am very much here*.

IF IT WAS HARD to find the beginning of this story, then it's also hard to decide on its end, and harder still to decide if there's any helpful lesson buried in all this experience. A very large part of my current self wishes that my younger self had eaten three meals a day, stayed home doing word puzzles, and gone to school like clockwork. I wish I hadn't smoked, done drugs, got so incredibly drunk, or run away. And I really wish I had not lost my virginity at thirteen. But underneath all this wishful thinking, I wonder – if I had not done these things, would I have been steadier, or happier, or safer? I don't know if I can ever answer that.

And perhaps the smoking and the drinking and the destruction are not the full story anyway. Perhaps a body of years should not be judged on the distillation of its most extreme moments. Perhaps I should have written about the tamer times, the TV nights, the family holidays, all those school essays I composed about *Hamlet*. And perhaps I should also have told you more about my life as it is now, to put it all in perspective, to show that I haven't just barely made it through – I have *flourished*. This is an important fact to know. My life is different now, and it's a good life. And so when you asked me yesterday how I was, and I said I was fine, that I was happy, I wasn't lying. I really meant it.

But I haven't told that story, and I haven't couched the story I have told in a cheerful context. I've only given you the bad bits. And in writing it this way, the bad bits become the whole story. So I pause, again, in the task of writing. I look at the notebook page, now so full of words, and crossings-out, and wonder if maybe I could write it differently? My internal critic says, 'Enough with the *negativity*, Emilie.' But then, just as I have that thought, I know that this has to be the story's shape.

These pages cover a period of about eight years. They contain many events and emotions that I have never told to anyone before, or even admitted to myself. The experience of writing them out has been very painful. That I cannot, or have not, avoided this pain by choosing not to write the story is due to one simple reason: the urge to write this feels not only dangerous and fearful and shameful, but necessary. I write this now to reclaim those parts of me that for so long I so thoroughly denied. I write it to unlock the code of silence that I kept for so many years. I write it so that I can, at last, feel present in my own life. I write it because it is the most powerful thing I can think of to do.

Finally, I write this because I can't time travel. For a long time I have had the recurring and sentimental wish that I could go back to the early 1990s and just hold on to my younger self, tightly, the way she needed, and not pay attention to her protestations that she was 'fine'. Because I know what I would say to her. I would embrace her and I would tell her that I know she is lonely, that I know she feels lost, that I know she feels worthless. And then, because she is not me, and because she is me, I would assure her that there *is* something about her, something amazing, something lovable, something special, something beautiful, something fragile, something strong, something worth fighting for.

THIS IS NOT ON
THE EXAM

GROWING UP, I HAD NO BICYCLE. Coincidentally, I had no friends either. And, just as I pretended I was fine hanging out by myself, I pretended I didn't care that I couldn't ride a bike. Then I got too old to start learning, too big for the baby bikes, and so that was it, I didn't learn. While other kids used their bikes to go out into the world, I stayed home reading. If I had to go somewhere, I walked. I told anyone who would listen that I didn't mind because I loved walking. I convinced even myself.

Then, in my thirties, when I moved by myself to another country, I thought I might revisit the whole bike thing. After all, if I failed, it wouldn't matter because no one would know. So I went to the local cycle shop and, in a tiny voice, asked if I could rent an adult bicycle with stabilisers. As soon as I said it, I wondered if such a thing even existed. But the bearded man behind the counter just nodded and asked me if I wanted to sign up for their adult learners' course, starting the following month. I blinked. I found it hard to imagine that there were any other adults who did not know how to ride a bike, let alone enough to run a course. Even so, I didn't want to wait. I asked again about renting a learner bike. The guy shook his head at stabilisers – but then he offered to give me one with the pedals taken off. I said I thought bicycles needed pedals to work. 'You need to learn to balance first,' he said, 'then graduate to pedalling.'

So I took the pedal-less bike he gave me, found an empty car park – with a slope – and started pushing myself along, first taking one foot off the ground, then, scarily, both. I did that for the whole morning, going round and round the car park. Once I got good at that, I pushed the bike a bit further up the slope. I turned. And then I halted, hands on the brakes, feet welded to the ground. It looked less like a slope now, more like quite a steep hill. Maybe I'd done enough for one day? Maybe I didn't really need to learn at all? But I knew the real failure would be to not even try. So I let go. And I glided, for the first time ever, I glided and I felt the air whoosh past me and the ground move under me. At the bottom of the hill, I skidded to a halt, terror giving way to amazement, amazement to pride. Then I pushed the bike back up to the top and let go again. All I did for the next two days was push myself and the bike to the top of the same small hill, letting go over and over. I was happy. I taught myself to ride a bike. I practically taught myself to fly. I recall that feeling of gliding and flying and whooshing now, and I wonder *what was I so frightened of*? And why can't I do that – just let go – more often?

WHEN I REALISED that I wanted to work as a university lecturer, I hoped that I would be the kind of teacher who would change students' lives, who would be profound, who would teach them things that would not be on the exam. I have tried to realise some of these ambitions by making my classroom a safe (and equal) space in which all of my students can take risks. Sometimes it seems that the biggest risk they can imagine is to say something out loud. I know that they are afraid of saying the wrong thing and being laughed at. But I want them to speak despite this fear. Because I worry that if students are quiet about their ideas in class perhaps they will be quiet about other things too. Things they should not be quiet about. If they cannot talk in class, how will they speak out if they get harassed, or discriminated against, or hurt?

I thought about this question when a student came to my office to ask about the end-of-term essay for my course. We had a lively conversation about the module and her ideas. She was smart and insightful and articulate. Yet in eight weeks I'd never heard her express an opinion during a seminar. 'Would you make these points next week in class?' I asked her. She mutely shook her head. 'You're really good,' I said. She looked surprised. And my heart sank. I knew this young woman was being quiet for a very particular reason: she is a girl and girls are taught to be quiet, taught that they are not good enough to be heard. The exceptional ones who risk saying something – anything – also risk being perceived as brash or arrogant. They were not born with these fears. They were not born feeling inferior. They were taught it. I know this because I was also taught it.

When I was twelve, I took entrance exams for a local school and I was awarded a scholarship. But when my mum read the school prospectus in detail, she realised that female pupils had to take a compulsory home economics course, whereas male pupils got extra maths lessons. The option for extra maths was not open to girls at all. My mother was unimpressed, so I did not go to that school. But the school I did end up going to discriminated against girls too. At the end of first year, weirdly, I scored 99% in two exams. Precociously, I asked both teachers what I had lost the 1% for. In each case, the teacher paused before answering. Then each said, as if scripted, that another pupil had done equally well but that only one of us could get 100%. They did not specify why I was not the 'one' but, in both cases, the other pupil was a boy. I got the message.

And in my job now I see the results of that message week after week, in class after class. Female students are so much more reticent than male students, because they are so much more likely to underestimate the worth of their contribution. At least, they usually are. That young woman, the quiet one with all the great ideas, was back in my class the following week. I began the discussion by asking the group for their general opinions on the play – had they liked it? There was a pause. Then she answered. She spoke once in that seminar, then two or three times in each seminar after that. And I admired her so much. Not because speaking out is hard. But because she was afraid and she did it anyway.

***

Notes to Self

I WORK IN A PROFESSION still very much dominated at the top by men. I myself have never been refused promotion, or sexually harassed at work, so in the main I'm doing fine. But the fact that the absence of these things makes me feel fortunate tells its own story. And the other side of that story is just how often I encounter casual sexism, which for all its superficiality, can be bruising. I have been talked down to and talked over and sometimes just ignored, all because I am female. I have been shouted at in meetings by senior male colleagues who rely on me not speaking back because I am junior and female. I have been called a 'feminazi'. Faced with these kinds of situations, what do other women do? What swift mental calculations do they perform? Do they challenge the shouting man? Do they laugh along at the sexist joke? Or do they, like me, side-step?

It was a photographer who called me a 'feminazi'. He was taking shots at a conference and directed me to cosy up to two male colleagues. When I hesitated, he let the insult fly. Beside me, the men laughed, nervously. Had either of them said anything, he would have been a feminist hero. If I'd said anything, I would have been a bitch. Though it was a man who had made the situation hostile, I was the woman, so I was expected to smooth it over, to smile for the camera, to be silent. And, heart-sinkingly, that's what I did.

Usually sexist comments in the workplace don't involve references to genocide, and this can make them easier to live with but also easier to miss. I have lost count of the number of times men, both older and younger than me, have told me that I look young. They act like it's a compliment, but it is so not a compliment. Women are meant to be flattered by being told we look young because, for a woman, looks are the most important thing, and youth is the best look of all. But in informing me that I look youthful, or that I don't understand because I'm too naive, or asking me if I'm a student when I am clearly a tenured lecturer, these men strip from me more than a decade of professional experience and expertise. The so-called compliment is, in fact, an instant demotion.

If you are female, if you are young, if you are subordinate, you do not have to be listened to. I only appreciated this fully late last year when I travelled overseas to give a guest lecture at another university. It was not a particularly cheerful lecture. I discussed several plays in which women testify about their experience of being raped. I talked about the difficulties that women have in speaking publicly about rape, and the taboos against women speaking publicly *at all* within certain cultures. I said that theatres are important spaces for women to find their voices and share their stories. After

I finished there was a brief silence. Sometimes I forget, when I get passionate about a subject, that even in an academic context the word 'rape' is rarely heard. I said I was happy to take questions.

The first comment came from a man who had earlier been introduced to me as the Chair of the Faculty. Starting slowly, he shook his head, and said that he wasn't sure how to respond. I'm used to this – when it comes to this difficult subject matter, I'm not always sure how to respond myself. I smiled to put him at his ease. Then he said, 'I find it hard to reconcile how you look and your manner with your subject matter. I mean you look . . . I don't want to use the word "cute" but . . .' He trailed off. He waved his hands towards me. Though he went on to ask a question, which I dutifully answered, he had set the tone for the discussion that followed. I was not to be taken seriously. Later that evening I described the event to a friend. Then, as an afterthought, I recalled the Faculty Chair. 'Oh yeah,' I said, 'this guy said the weirdest thing, he called me "cute." ' My friend shuddered. And it was only then that I admitted to myself how angry I was at being judged on what I looked like, not on what I said. But then, as my anger died, a new emotion replaced it: shame. I had not objected.

The stinging irony, of course, was that my entire talk

was about the ways that women are intimidated into silence. And here I was, with a platform to speak, finding myself with the same difficulty. The Faculty Chair's comment implied that I shouldn't be talking about rape. It is more than just tedious, this women-should-be-seen-but-not-heard attitude. It is a way of telling women to get back to where they belong, back to being silent. I am gobsmacked that I still encounter this attitude in the university. And I am, most of all, weary of having to come up with something in response. I should have laughed outright at the Faculty Chairman. I should have called him on his misogyny. But in the moment that he said it, I did not even allow myself to think about the implications of his comment. I wanted to look professional. I wanted to seem strong. I wanted to move on. And so I side-stepped. Which is, of course, a kind of silence.

It's funny to describe myself as silent because I'm actually pretty loud. I get asked to make announcements at events because I can be heard above the din. A friend of mine once told me I barely needed a mobile phone because I could just shout and be heard from miles away. And I'm loud in other ways too. I speak up at meetings, I contribute to discussions, and hey, get this, my job as a lecturer means that *I talk for a living*. But you can be silent and loud at the same time, it turns out.

Though I have no fear of speaking publicly, or of being perceived as ambitious, both of which are classic stumbling blocks for professional women, I am prey to an equally treacherous problem: I give away my power. In side-stepping, in not calling out the sexist remarks, I act as if they are in the right, I act as if women should not have voices, and I act as if I am not a feminist. And the truth is, I am tired of being a feminist. I am tired of it being women's responsibility to identify *and* tackle *and* fix sexism. I am tired of it being so necessary and so difficult. And I am tired of my own acts of internalising, tired of my complicity, tired of playing the game.

LET ME TAKE ANOTHER SIDEWAYS STEP HERE and tell you something I learned about myself this past year or so. Are you ready? I don't care about your feelings. I don't even know you, but I don't care how you're feeling, what you're feeling, even if you have feelings at all. Why? Because, apparently, I lack empathy.

This may not come as a surprise to some but it came as one to me. It started after I did a test at work about empathetic listening and got alarming results. I did a different test. But the results were still terrible. So then I signed up for one-to-one personality testing. I sat in a small room with an HR consultant and a pile of flash cards. She asked me to imagine a series of scenarios and respond. If someone, say, told me their house was broken into, would I commiserate, make them a cup of tea, ask them how it happened, or advise them on lock-smiths? Obviously, I said, the correct thing is to give them the number of a locksmith. 'Hmm,' she said. Time after time, I gave the non-empathetic answer. At the end of the session, the HR consultant told me that I have an admirable approach – I try to solve problems, ask logical questions, ascertain the facts. But I do not, she broke it gently, have empathy. 'Well, of course not,' I said defensively, 'I'm at work. I'm not meant to be empathetic at work.'

The consultant smiled, in a practised, non-judgemental way, and asked me why I thought feelings had no place at work. She said vulnerability could be a kind of strength. I felt a hurricane in my brain. I was remembering a few years ago when I had desperately wanted to share my feelings at work, but had silenced myself.

I had been asked to present during my department's research day, to talk about my current work. I didn't think I should give a presentation, because I hadn't done anything spectacular, but the organiser said people would be interested, and he reiterated the request. So I said yes. I regretted saying yes in the lead-up to speaking. I regretted it during, and afterwards too. I regretted it because even though the project I was working on was good, I was a mess. It was nearly Christmas. I had recently moved house. I had unrelenting insomnia. And I had just had a miscarriage. I'd told no one at work about the pregnancy, save my boss. I was tired and I was numb. So I gave a vague and unimpressive talk, extolling the benefits of 'putting our research out there'. But all I really wanted to say was that I felt sad.

I see now that saying I felt sad would have been a worthwhile contribution. Not because my sadness warranted attention, but because, though we were all close colleagues, none of us was discussing the emotions we bring to our jobs, and the emotions we generate through our work. Instead we were busy impressing each other with our professionalism and our ambitions and our achievements. And looking back, I think that was dishonest. Yes, it might have been weird for me to say I felt sad – and that's precisely why I didn't do it – but it might also have enabled us to talk about how teaching and research can give us something else, different emotions, can make us feel capable, valuable, and meaningful. That range of feeling was worth claiming, worth talking about. But I didn't claim it, and I didn't talk about it, for one reason. Because to say I felt sad would have been dangerously feminine.

When I examine my antipathy to emotion at work, I realise that I think feelings – having them, showing them, talking about them – are not just a sign of femininity, but a sign of weakness. I have internalised the idea that to be taken seriously as an intellectual, I have to deny all those feelings, all that femininity, all that weakness. I think this in spite of myself, and in spite of my feminism – and all the women on my reading lists, and all the women-forward events I organise, and all my research on women speaking out, and all my criticism of 'manels', and all the posters on my office door advertising marches for reproductive rights. Because, it turns out, I am sexist too.

This lesson was driven home to me during a recent leadership course aimed at women working at universities in Ireland. We all met one February morning in an overheated basement conference room, to learn how to 'get ahead'. One of the first exercises was for each participant to identify a role model. I thought about who I would pick, and what my choice would mean for the kind of person I wanted to be. I picked a female professor whose work I admire hugely and who is a great public intellectual and speaker. But in the next part of the task, discussing our role models within our small groups, I was amazed, as the discussion moved around the table, that the majority of women in my group had chosen their mothers. Their reasons all centred on the fortitude, moral strength, and selflessness of these women – they were the heroic qualities they wanted to emulate. I was angry about all these mothers. All I could think was that here we were at a professional event, aimed at helping women break down barriers in their career paths and yet all these women were saying they wanted to be like their mums. *No wonder you can't get promoted*, I thought, meanly, *if your role model stayed home*.

Here's the thing: my mother worked long hours out of the home. She taught me that the most important thing for a woman is to be financially independent. She taught me that women should be ambitious and take pride in their work. She taught me that work comes first and the domestic, with all its feelings, comes second. All these lessons conditioned me to think of working as the brave and necessary journey that women must take. So, ironically, I could have claimed my mother as my role model. But I would *never* have said 'my mum' when they asked about role models, because I couldn't have put motherhood at the top of the hierarchy of achievements. Because the qualities I generally associate with motherhood – love and support, empathy and nurturing – are not those I associate with being successful at work. And there's that internalised sexism again.

I HAVE ALWAYS WANTED TO BE LIKED. In this, I am no different to other women. Women want to be likeable. Women are *supposed* to be likeable. Women are judged when they are not likeable enough. But being likeable, for all its social desirability, held us back at work. We ended up so busy doing all the pastoral care, and all the boring paperwork, and all the millions of unwanted jobs, that we never seemed to have time to ask for recognition. And, if we did ask, we were held back again. We were told we should be less kind-hearted, less compromising, less *nice*. After all, nice girls don't get the corner office. Men got promoted ahead of women because they, of course, were bold, daring, uncompromising; all those coded ways of saying that men didn't need to bother about being likeable because they were too busy being powerful.

The ways things are now, though, *everyone* needs to be likeable, because these days the career ladder – for men as well as women – is indistinguishable from the esteem ladder, the *how-much-your-employer-likes-you* ladder. This ladder is hard to climb because the likeability goalposts keep moving. At my university, sometimes they want you to publish more. Sometimes they want you to teach more. Sometimes they want you to do more admin. If you want to be really liked, it's all three. And, just as with all that niceness, there's a hitch to all this likeability. The more we do, the more we are esteemed. But then the more we do, the more they want us to do. And then the more they want us 'to improve performance and deliver success'. And ultimately, in a cash-strapped, do-more-with-less university, success means bringing in money.

I receive two emails a week on applying for funding. Two emails, that's easy to ignore, right? But then there's the third email. The weekly President's Bulletin, which includes a list of all the people in the university who have been awarded external funding. This is how we all get the message. Yay for the overworkers! Yay for the financially successful few! Boo for the rest! I could try to shake it off, I could find other markers of esteem. But I want to be liked. So when I realised that only money got you really liked, I started to read the funding emails and I clicked on the links and I rethought the potential of my research to deliver grant cheques. And when I got a project funded I celebrated, because here was proof – I was likeable.

But this is not a humble brag, it is an instructive fable. When I applied for funding three years ago, I did not understand that I was, effectively, also applying for a new job. With the award came the responsibility to lead a project team, to manage a budget of hundreds of thousands of euro, to produce 'high-impact outputs'. I was not trained for this, but I rationalised, 'I'm tough, I can rise to the challenge.' Still, although the funding bought me out of teaching, I did not relinquish any of my other responsibilities. So now I had two jobs. And then I said yes to even more. I took on the editorship of a journal. I bargained my way into writing two books under contract, ignoring the fact that the due dates for both were in the same month. I signed up for international conferences. I organised three conferences myself. I travelled so much that I actually started to *collect air miles*. And I smiled when friends and colleagues asked me if I ever slept, because this – *this* – was what success looked like. But really, it was what being a workaholic looked like.

Why did I become a workaholic? The expectations for overwork were certainly management's. But that can't be the only reason. Because the expectations for perfection were mine. When I could not get pregnant again after my miscarriage, I told myself that I had failed at having children. I said it over and over, as if conception were an exam that I could have studied harder for. Unable to be a mother, I decided that I would define myself through my job instead. I can see in hindsight that this was a mistake, as instead of grieving I threw myself more and more into my work. But even in hindsight I can't work out why it went quite so wrong, why trying to be good at my job led me to be so unkind to myself.

From the outside I looked fine: performing an image of success – book contract! funded project! journal! But in reality I was having a silent breakdown. A minor breakdown, as they go, but nonetheless a breaking down. I was working every weekend and, consumed with my job, I stopped returning texts from friends. The times my boyfriend suggested going for a bike ride, I would snap back that I was too busy. And though my work consists of activities that I love – teaching, researching, writing – the mounting pressure of constant deadlines was killing my love of them, and of myself. I stopped being just sad, and I started being depressed. I did not read depression as a danger signal, I did not step off the treadmill, and I did not get help.

I thought that my depression was a sign of character weakness. I thought that if I could only stop wasting so much time being sad, I would be more productive.

I worked longer hours to disguise the depression. Sometimes I was so tired and so sad that I would lock my office door, turn off the light and lie on the floor. I felt like I was being smothered with a blanket of anxiety. The smallest tasks felt like they would defeat me and I beat myself up for the tiniest mistake. I looked at other people, who didn't seem to be drowning the way I was, and wondered how they did it. When a colleague told me that she began her research work at 9pm, after the kids were in bed, I didn't feel pity for her – I was jealous of her discipline.

And then last summer, at the encouragement of the research office, and because I'm such a good girl, I took on another funding application. As I agreed to do it, I told myself it would only mean a month's work, overlooking the fact that I would have to work every day of the month without a break. When I told my family I was applying for another big grant they each said, 'Don't do it.' And then, when I ignored that advice, they each said, 'Well, I hope you don't get it.' And almost as soon as the application was underway, I realised they were right, it was a mistake. How did I get into this, I wondered, but it was far too late. I strategised and consulted and drafted and redrafted until I thought my brain would melt. And, of course, I kept doing my regular job too. In taking on yet more work, I was the architect of my own breakdown. But I was not alone on this road – the university was cheerleading me all the way to crazytown. Yay for the overworkers!

IT ALL BEGAN TO FALL APART at the start of the conference season. I was travelling to a symposium in late June, the day was hot and I was distracted leaving the house. I was in the airport before I realised I had forgotten my jacket. Ordinarily no big deal, but I was flying to Norway and the weather forecast was ominous: cold and wet. As I stood in Departures, without any warm clothes whatsoever, what should have been a slapstick moment felt like a catastrophic mistake. In the throes of a panic attack, heart beating, sweat pouring, breath short, I phoned my boyfriend. He listened, then calmed and reassured me. He suggested I buy a jacket at the airport. I bought the warmest one I could find and I wore it, gratefully, all through the conference. Crisis averted.

Two days later there was another hitch. My flight home was cancelled. Though it was only Friday afternoon, the airline said they couldn't get me out of the country until Sunday. But that couldn't be right, because I had to give a lecture in Frankfurt on Monday. I panicked again. At first, I tried cajoling the staff. Then I started to shout. I demanded to speak to the supervisor. She arrived but only told me, again, that there were no flights. Then I noticed the wedding ring on her finger and, guessing she might be a mother, I tried a new tactic: I showed her the picture of my nephew on my phone screensaver. I said he was my son, and that I had to get home for him. *I had tears in my eyes*. She looked at the photo, at me, then turned back to the desk and picked up the phone. As she rerouted me to fly out on Saturday I tried to keep the triumphant grin from my face. Crisis averted. Again. I barely slept that night. In the morning I took the first flight out, one of three planes I would have to get on that day. Traipsing around the airports of Europe was exhausting. But – and this was the thing – I actually felt happier than I had in ages. I was high on the hypomania of working, working, working. 'Nothing can stop me,' I thought, as I tapped away at my laptop first in Stavanger, then Aberdeen, then Schiphol. Superwoman.

On Monday, still in a fug of tiredness, I flew to Frankfurt, gave my lecture, then flew home. The next day, though I barely knew what time zone I was in, I hauled myself back to work to finish the funding application. I pressed 'submit' with shaking fingers. I left my office and stood, momentarily confused, gazing down the shadowy and silent corridor. I was the only person left in the building. Obsessed with completing the application, I had not noticed the time, and though it was midsummer, the sky outside was dark. I realised I was hungry. I thought back and I could not remember the last time I ate an actual meal. At least, I consoled myself, it's over now, I can go back to normal. Crisis averted – really and truly this time.

But how many times can you avert a crisis before you admit it's all one long crisis? The next evening I drove my car into a wall. I was on my way to pick my nephew up, to help my sister out, to give her a break from being a single parent. As I arrived at her house, I turned the car, but I was so spaced out that I did not see the gatepost. Suddenly there was the sound of scraping and scrunching as metal crumpled. My first thought was for my nephew, but, thankfully, he was nowhere near. Then I thought about the wall, and the car, cringing at the damage. Only slowly did I begin to wonder if I was alright. I was hugging the wheel. I was almost crying. And my whole body was trembling with adrenaline, trembling because I had confirmed what I knew. I knew something bad was coming down the track. I knew that I would break something. And now I had – I'd broken the car. And I was *elated*. Because I had thought the thing that would get broken was me.

I may not have much empathy for others but, in fairness, I have none for myself either. I knew I was taking on too much and, at some level, I knew I was miserable. That's not to say there weren't plenty of times in the last two years that I was happy. But when you're exhausted and depressed there is a strange divide. You know you should be feeling happy, you can tell yourself, 'Now I am happy,' but the experience is somehow artificial, unreal. I stood on the edges of my emotions. And I stood on the edges of myself. And I couldn't tell anyone. Because to have told anyone, to have said the word 'depressed' out loud, would have been the ultimate failure. I knew something was going to break. And I didn't care.

AT THE BEGINNING of the stress-bonanza years, I took a one-day 'Mindfulness for Academics' course. There were about twenty people in the room, and every one of us voiced the same issue: our jobs are too stressful. In hindsight, we needed less work, not more mindfulness. But since less work didn't even feel like an option, we were trying to 'fix' ourselves instead, to be more resilient in the face of the onslaught. Really we were cannibalising ourselves. Or the university was cannibalising us, I'm not sure which.

There is no mechanism for me to go to the people who run the university and say, 'Hey, you know what, guys' – and it is, mostly, guys – 'it might be time to tell your employees to slow down.' That memo will never get sent. In fact, I can't even *imagine* it being sent. In acknowledging this, I don't really blame the austerity-hit university for trying to turn its employees into revenue hunters and, as a consequence, sucking us dry. Well, okay, I do. But my mental health, it turns out, is my responsibility. I probably don't need to tell you that, but I did need to tell myself. And once I realised that, I wondered why I would ever leave it in the hands of strangers to decide my value.

After the car crash, I did not transform myself overnight. And though I am trying to be different, many of the problems I describe here still mark my life. 'So, what *has* changed?' a friend asked me recently. And here is the answer: these days I have a new to-do list. Actually, it's not a to-do list. It's more like a series of notes to self.

I will value my ideas and my feelings. I will write every day because writing is one of the things that make me feel most alive. I will lecture on and teach what I am passionate about. I will not hesitate to say the word 'rape' out loud just because I am wearing a nice skirt. I will call out misogyny. I will fight the internalised sexism. I will be kind to my colleagues precisely because I don't know what, or how, they are feeling. I will eat breakfast. I will eat lunch. I will eat dinner (and not at my desk). I will pay attention to my middle-aged body. I will spend time with the people I love. I will be a daughter and a sister and an aunt and a partner and a friend. And I will ask my students what they would do, if they were not afraid. And I will listen to what they say. And I will remind them, with compassion, that the real failure is to not try.

I am trying. And I am afraid. I am afraid to write about side-stepping and feelings and overwork and depression and breakdown because I am still convinced that admitting vulnerability makes me seem weak, not strong. I am afraid of confirming that I am young and cute and powerless. I am afraid of admitting to all the hard stuff, all the bad stuff, all the unlikeable stuff. I am afraid of exposing myself. I am afraid of being pitied. Of being resented. Of being shouted at. I am afraid of being the disruptive woman. And of not being disruptive enough.

I am afraid. But I am doing it anyway.

Acknowledgements

Without Lisa Coen and Sarah Davis-Goff *Notes to Self* would not exist, and I would like to thank them for their vision and inspiration, and their editorial interventions. My thanks also to Karolina Sutton at Curtis Brown, and Simon Prosser and Hamish Hamilton. I am also very grateful to the friends and colleagues who helped me believe I could – should – write this book.

In these essays, I have tried not to tell anyone else's story, but only to tell mine as truthfully as possible. Inevitably, though, I have strayed into the stories and experiences of my family. A heartfelt thank you to my sister, and my parents, for their generous and gracious support despite my acts of trespass.

And, finally, there would be no words without R.

He just wanted a decent book to read ...

Not too much to ask, is it? It was in 1935 when Allen Lane, Managing Director of Bodley Head Publishers, stood on a platform at Exeter railway station looking for something good to read on his journey back to London. His choice was limited to popular magazines and poor-quality paperbacks – the same choice faced every day by the vast majority of readers, few of whom could afford hardbacks. Lane's disappointment and subsequent anger at the range of books generally available led him to found a company – and change the world.

'We believed in the existence in this country of a vast reading public for intelligent books at a low price, and staked everything on it'
Sir Allen Lane, 1902–1970, founder of Penguin Books

The quality paperback had arrived – and not just in bookshops. Lane was adamant that his Penguins should appear in chain stores and tobacconists, and should cost no more than a packet of cigarettes.

Reading habits (and cigarette prices) have changed since 1935, but Penguin still believes in publishing the best books for everybody to enjoy. We still believe that good design costs no more than bad design, and we still believe that quality books published passionately and responsibly make the world a better place.

So wherever you see the little bird – whether it's on a piece of prize-winning literary fiction or a celebrity autobiography, political tour de force or historical masterpiece, a serial-killer thriller, reference book, world classic or a piece of pure escapism – you can bet that it represents the very best that the genre has to offer.

Whatever you like to read – trust Penguin.